T0363857

STORYFUN

5

TEACHER'S BOOK

Second edition

Karen Saxby
Emily Hird

Cambridge University Press
www.cambridge.org/elt

Cambridge Assessment English
www.cambridgeenglish.org

Information on this title: www.cambridge.org/9781316617274

© Cambridge University Press and UCLES 2017

First published 2011 © Cambridge University Press
Second edition 2017 © Cambridge University Press and UCLES

20 19 18 17 16 15 14 13 12 11 10 9 8 7

Printed in Great Britain by CPI Group (UK) Ltd, Croydon CR0 4YY

A catalogue record for this publication is available from the British Library

ISBN 978-1-316-61724-3 Student's Book with online activities and Home Fun booklet 5
ISBN 978-1-316-61727-4 Teacher's Book with Audio 5
ISBN 978-1-316-61732-8 Presentation plus 5

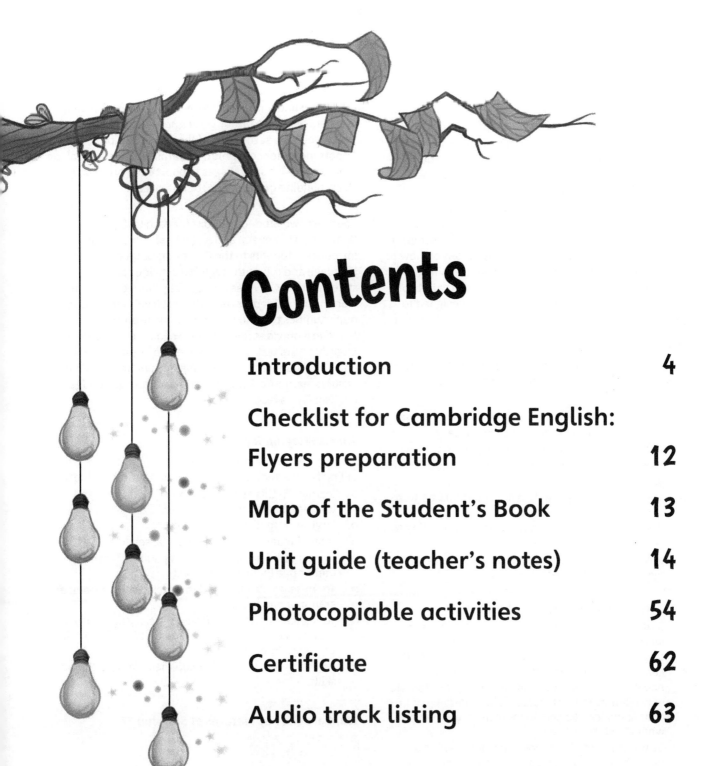

Contents

Introduction 4

Checklist for Cambridge English: Flyers preparation 12

Map of the Student's Book 13

Unit guide (teacher's notes) 14

Photocopiable activities 54

Certificate 62

Audio track listing 63

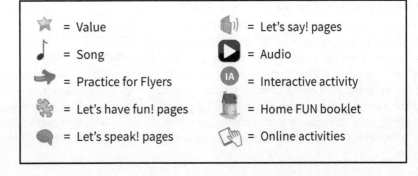

☆ = Value		🔊 = Let's say! pages	
♪ = Song		▶ = Audio	
➡ = Practice for Flyers		IA = Interactive activity	
✳ = Let's have fun! pages		🏠 = Home FUN booklet	
💬 = Let's speak! pages		👆 = Online activities	

Introduction

Welcome to *Storyfun*!

Storyfun is a series of six books written for young learners aged between 6 and 12 years. The series provides story-based preparation for the Cambridge English: Young Learners tests (YLE). Each Student's Book contains eight stories with activities that include vocabulary and grammar tasks, puzzles, games, poems, songs and an exploration of the story 'value' (for example, an appreciation of nature, the importance of friendship). The Teacher's Books provide detailed suggestions on how to approach the storytelling, together with clear instructions for guiding learners through the unit. With a variety of flexible resources, each unit in *Storyfun* is designed to provide approximately three to four hours of class time.

Why stories?

Storyfun aims to provide an opportunity for language practice by engaging learners' interest in stories.

Research has shown that meaningful and imaginative stories can motivate learning because learners:

o engage with the text and their imaginations.
o learn vocabulary with repetition of key words in the text and pictures.
o are exposed to repeated rhyme and sound patterns and accurate pronunciation.
o develop deeper social understanding by relating to characters and events in the story.
o actively engage listening skills as they predict, hypothesise and await outcomes.

Points to remember for effective learning:

o Story-reading should be interactive (teacher and learners). It should involve pointing, describing and discussing how the story relates to the real world.
o Learners will engage with a story more if they are encouraged to 'work out' the meaning, for example, why learners think characters did something or how characters felt at a certain moment and, of course, what the story 'value' is.
o Learners benefit from more than one reading or hearing of a story. At least one reading should be read/heard right the way through from beginning to end without interruption.

For more information about stories in language learning, go to

Why Cambridge English: Young Learners (YLE)?

The stories have been written to reflect the different language levels and topic areas of the Cambridge English: Starters, Movers and Flyers tests and to appeal to the target-reader age groups. The language of the stories is exploited in activities that check comprehension, teach key vocabulary and grammar, practise all four language skills (reading, writing, listening and speaking) and give learners an opportunity to familiarise themselves with the nature and format of the Cambridge English: Young Learners tests. The optional *Let's have fun!* and *Let's speak!* sections at the back of the books also provide opportunities for collaborative learning and test speaking practice. The *Let's say!* pages support early pronunciation skills, building from sounds to sentences.

There are two Student's Books for each test: pre-A1 (Starters), A1 (Movers) and A2 (Flyers). *Storyfun 5* gently introduces students to the Cambridge English: Flyers language and topics through fun activities and test-style practice. Activities are carefully graded to ensure learners are guided towards the test level, with frequent opportunities to build up their language and skills. *Storyfun 6* provides full examples of all the Cambridge English: Flyers test tasks. By the end of *Storyfun* levels 5 and 6, constant recycling of language and test task types ensures learners are fully prepared for the Cambridge English: Flyers test.

Who is *Storyfun* for?

Storyfun has been written for teachers and young learners of English in a wide variety of situations. It is suitable for:

o learners in this age group who enjoy reading and listening to stories
o large and small groups of learners
o monolingual and multilingual classes
o learners who are beginning preparation for the Cambridge English: Flyers test
o young learners who need to develop their vocabulary, grammar and language
o young learners keen to discuss social values, develop collaborative learning skills and build confidence for the Flyers Speaking paper
o teachers who wish to develop their learners' literacy skills

What are the key features of *Storyfun 5*?

Student's Book

o eight imaginative and motivating stories
o fun, interactive, creative and meaningful activities
o activities similar to task types found in all three parts (Reading and Writing, Listening and Speaking) of the Cambridge English: Flyers test

- an introduction to Cambridge English: Flyers grammar and vocabulary
- extension activities *Let's have fun!*, further speaking practice *Let's speak!* and an early pronunciation focus *Let's say!*
- a unit-by-unit word list

Home FUN booklet

- fun activities for learners to try at home
- 'self-assessment' activities that build learners' confidence and encourage autonomy
- a Cambridge English: Flyers picture dictionary
- *Let's have fun!* pages to encourage learners to use English in the wider world
- answers, audio and additional support found online by using the access code at the front of the book

Teacher's Book with Audio

- a map of the Student's Book (topics, grammar points and Flyers test practice for each unit)
- practical step-by-step notes with suggestions for:

  - ✓ personalisation at presentation and practice stages
  - ✓ skills work: reading, writing, listening, speaking, drawing and colouring
  - ✓ pair and group work
  - ✓ puzzles, games, poems and songs
  - ✓ speaking activities and projects
  - ✓ discussion tasks to explore the story 'value'
  - ✓ recycling of language
  - ✓ incorporating digital materials into the lesson

- Cambridge English: Flyers test tips
- full audioscripts
- imaginative audio recordings for stories and activities (downloadable by using the access code at the front of this book) reflective of the Cambridge English: Flyers Listening test
- photocopiable pages for the Student's Book or optional extension activities
- links to online practice and the Home FUN booklet

Presentation plus

- digital version of all Student's Book pages
- interactive Student's Book activities
- audio played directly from the digital page
- digital flashcards with audio
- digital slideshow of every story
- an Image carousel that provides further visuals associated with story themes
- integrated tools to make notes and highlight activities

Online Practice

For the Teacher
- Presentation plus
- All audio recordings
- Additional digital resources to support your classes

For the Student
- Fun activities to practise the exam, skills and language
- All audio recordings
- Additional digital resources

Word FUN World app

- Cambridge English: Young Learners vocabulary game
- For mobile phones and tablets

Storytelling

Why should we use stories in language learning classes?

There are several reasons! A good story encourages us to turn the next page and read more. We want to find out what happens next and what the main characters do and say to each other. We may feel excited, sad, afraid, angry or really happy. The experience of reading or listening to a story is likely to make us 'feel' that we are part of the story, too. Just like in our 'real' lives, we might love or hate different characters. Perhaps we recognise ourselves or other people we know in some of the story characters. Perhaps they have similar talents, ambitions, weaknesses or problems.

Because of this natural connection with story characters, our brains process the reading of stories differently from the way we read factual information. This is because our brains don't always recognise the difference between an imagined situation and a real one so the characters become 'alive' to us. What they say or do is therefore <u>much more meaningful</u>. The words and structures that relate a story's events, descriptions and conversations are processed by learners in a deeper way.

Encouraging learners to read or listen to stories should therefore help them to learn a second language in a way that is not only fun, but memorable.

How else do stories help?

Stories don't only offer the young reader a chance to learn more vocabulary and develop their grammatical skills. The experience also creates an opportunity to develop critical and creative thinking, emotional literacy and social skills. As learners read a story, they will be imagining far more details than its words communicate. Each learner will, subconsciously, be 'animating' the characters and making judgements and predictions about events.

As a teacher, you can encourage creativity and critical thinking by asking learners in groups to develop characters in more detail, talk about the part of the story they enjoyed most/least or even write different endings. You can also discuss, in English or L1 if necessary, the story 'values', in other words, what different stories teach us about how to relate to others.

Stories also offer a forum for personalised learning. No two learners will feel exactly the same about a story and an acceptance of difference can also be interesting to explore and discuss in class.

How can we encourage learners to join in and ask parents to help?

If, at first, learners lack confidence or motivation to read stories in English, help by reading the story to them without stopping so learners are just enjoying the story, stress free, and following as well as they can by looking at the pictures. During a second reading you might encourage interaction by asking questions like *Is this funny, scary or sad?* (Starters) *Was that a good idea?* (Movers) *What do you think will happen next?* (Flyers). If the class is read to in a relaxed and fun way, learners will subconsciously relate to the reading and language learning process more confidently and positively. Of course, being read to by a parent at home, too, is also simply a lovely way to share quiet and close time. To engage parents in the language learning process, you might share some of the above points with them or encourage them to search online for language learning activities to do at home with their children.

The Home FUN booklet has been specially designed for learners to use at home with parents. Activities are fun and easy to follow, requiring little instruction. The booklet aims to help learners show parents what they have learnt at school and to engage them in the learning process.

Further suggestions for storytelling

○ Involve learners in the topic and ask guessing and prediction questions in L1 if necessary. This will engage learners in the process of storytelling and motivate learning. When you pause the audio during the story, ask learners …

  ➢ about the topic and themselves
  ➢ to guess aspects of the story
  ➢ to say how they think a character feels or what they may say next

○ If you are telling the story yourself, support your learners in any way you can by adding your own dramatisation. For instance, you can read the stories with as much animation as possible and use props such as puppets or soft toys and different voices to bring the stories to life.

○ Incorporate the use of realia into the storytelling process. For example, if you are using *Storyfun 5*, in 'Ben's wishes' you could bring in props like bowls, spoons and books for learners to use when role playing the story, and in 'Treasure' you could bring in things you would take to the beach.

○ Once learners are familiar with the story they could even act out parts of the story in role plays. This will not only involve learners in the stories and add a fun element but can also help in practising and consolidating language.

Suggestions for using the story pictures

For skills practice

○ Before listening to the story, learners look at all the pictures on the story pages and discuss in small groups who or what they think the story is about and what the key events are.

○ Learners trace a picture (adding their own choice of extra details) and then follow your colouring or drawing instructions.

To encourage creative thinking

○ Groups choose two people in a picture and imagine what they are saying to each other. They then write a question with answer or a short dialogue.

○ Groups choose a background person in a picture and invent details about him/her. For example, how old they are, what they like doing, where they live, what pet they have.

○ Groups invent details that are unseen in the picture, for example, ten things in a bag, cupboard or garden.

○ Learners imagine they are 'in' the picture. What is behind / in front of / next to them? What can they feel (the sun, a cold wind …), smell (flowers, cooking …) or hear (birds, traffic …)?

To revise vocabulary and grammar

o Learners find as many things in a picture as they can which begin with a particular letter, for example, f.

o Learners list things in a picture that are a certain colour or in a certain place. For example, what someone is wearing or what is on the table.

o Learners choose four things they can see in a picture and list the words according to the size of the object or length of the word. Learners could also choose things according to categories such as food or animals.

o Using the pictures to revise grammar, for example *This is / These are*.

o Choose a picture in the story and ask learners in groups to say what is happening in this part of the story.

o Practise prepositions by asking learners what they can see in a picture in different places, for example, in the box, on the table or under the tree.

o Practise question forms by asking learners about different aspects of a picture, for example: *What colour is the cat? How many ducks are there? What's the boy doing?*

o On the board, write the first and last letter of four things learners can remember in a particular story picture. Learners complete the words.

o Point to objects or people in a picture and ask *This/These yes/no* questions. For example: *Is this a shoe? Are these toys? Is this a boy? Are these hats?*

o Ask *yes/no* colour and *how many* questions. For example, point to an apple and ask *Is this apple blue? Can you see four apples?*

o Show learners a story picture for 30 seconds and then ask *What's in that picture?* Write learners' answers on the board.

o Ask simple *What's the word* questions and build on known vocabulary sets. For example: *It's green. You can eat it. It's a fruit.* (a pear / an apple / a grape / a kiwi)

Suggestions for using the word list

At the back of the Student's Book, learners will find a list of important Flyers words that appear in each unit.

o Play 'Which word am I?' Learners work in pairs, looking at the word list for the unit. Choose a noun and give the class clues about it until one pair guesses it. Don't make the clues too easy and focus on form first and meaning afterwards. Say, for example: *I've got four letters. The letter 'k' is in me. You can sit on me. You can ride me to school.* (bike)

o Divide the class into A and B pairs. Learner A sits facing the board. Learner B sits with his/her back to the board. Write four words (nouns or verbs are best) from the word list for the unit on the board. Learner A then draws or mimes them until their partner guesses them all and writes them correctly (with the help of Learner A who can only say *Yes, that's right!* or *No, that's wrong!*). When everyone has finished, learners change places. Write some new words on the board. Learner B in each pair mimes these words for Learner A to guess.

o Play 'Tell me more, please!' Choose a noun from the word list for the unit and write it on the board, for example: *banana*. Learners take turns to add more information about the banana. For example, Learner A says: *The banana is long.* Learner B adds: *The banana is long. It's yellow.* Learner C says: *The banana is long. It's yellow. It's a fruit.* Continue until learners can't remember previous information.

o Pairs work together to make as many words from the word list for the unit as they can, using a number of letters that you dictate to the class. Alternatively, use word tiles from board games or letter cards made by the class. These could also be used for spelling tests in pairs or groups.

o On the board, write eight words from the word list for the unit with the letters jumbled. Pairs work as fast as they can to find the words and spell them correctly.

o On the board, write eight words from the word list for the unit. Spell three or four of them incorrectly. Pairs work as fast as they can to identify the misspelt words (they shouldn't be told how many there are) and to write them down correctly.

o Play 'Make a word'. Each group chooses a word (four, five or six letters long) from the word list for the unit and creates it by forming a human sculpture, i.e. learners in each group stand in a line, using their arms or legs to create the shapes of each letter. Remember you may need two learners for some letters (e.g. *k*). When all the groups are ready, the words are guessed.

o Use the word list for the unit to play common word games such as hangman, bingo and definition games or for dictated spelling tests. A nice alternative to the traditional hangman, which learners may enjoy, is an animal with its mouth open, with 8–10 steps leading down into its mouth. (You could use a crocodile at Starters, a shark at Movers or a dinosaur at Flyers.) With each incorrect guess, the stick person falls down onto the next step, and gets eaten if they reach the animal's mouth!

For more information on Cambridge English: Young Learners, please visit. From here, you can download the handbook for teachers, which includes information about each level of the Young Learners tests. You can also find information for candidates and their parents, including links to videos of the Speaking test at each level. There are also sample test papers, as well as further games and songs and links to the Teaching Support website.

A few final classroom points

Please try to be as encouraging as possible when working through the activities. By using phrases such as *Now you! You choose! Well done! Don't worry!* you are also helping learners to feel more confident about participating fully in the class and trying hard to do their best. Make sure that everyone in your class adds to open class work, however minimally, and when mistakes are made, view them as opportunities for learning. Try not to interrupt to correct learners during open class discussion, role plays, etc. Doing so might negatively affect a child's willingness to contribute in future. It takes courage to speak out in class. Make mental notes of mistakes and then cover them at a later moment with the whole class.

Have fun!

But most of all, please remember that an hour's lesson can feel very much longer than that to a learner who feels excluded, fearful of making mistakes, unsure about what to do, unable to follow instructions or express any personal opinions. An hour's lesson will feel like five minutes if a learner is having fun, sensing their own progress and participating fully in enjoyable and meaningful activities.

How is the Student's Book organised?

Story

Four illustrated story pages using language (topics, vocabulary and grammar) needed for the Cambridge English: Flyers test.

Vocabulary activity

Each unit of four-page activities opens with a vocabulary comprehension activity related to the key Cambridge English: Flyers vocabulary presented in the story.

Value key phrase

A key English phrase within the story demonstrates the story 'value'. For example, *Working as a team* ➔ "Good thinking!"

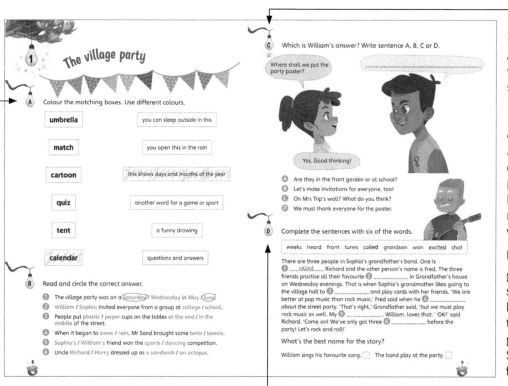

Skills

All activities develop reading, writing, listening and speaking skills useful for the YLE tests.

⭐ **Value activities** encourage learners to think about the story in a social context and practise the key phrase. The phrase aids learners to contextualise, remember and demonstrate the value in English.

Practice for Flyers activities

gently introduce learners to the style of the Cambridge English: Flyers test tasks and cover the key skills, vocabulary and grammar necessary for the test. See ➔ in the Teacher's Book for identification.

♪ Songs

Open activities such as poems and songs maintain learners' motivation and interest.

❋ Let's have fun!

Optional projects or games at the back of the Student's Book promote collaborative learning.

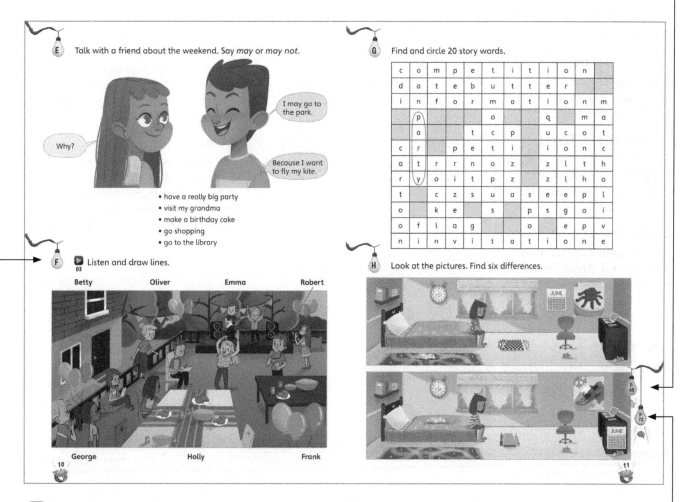

E Talk with a friend about the weekend. Say *may* or *may not*.

Why?

I may go to the park.

Because I want to fly my kite.

- have a really big party
- visit my grandma
- make a birthday cake
- go shopping
- go to the library

F 🔊 Listen and draw lines.
03

Betty   Oliver   Emma   Robert

George   Holly   Frank

10

G Find and circle 20 story words.

c	o	m	p	e	t	i	t	i	o	n	
d	a	t	e	b	u	t	t	e	r		
i	n	f	o	r	m	a	t	i	o	n	m
	p				o		q		m	a	
	a		t	c	p		u	c	o	t	
c	r		p	e	t	i		i	o	n	c
a	t	r	r	n	o	z		z	l	t	h
r	y	o	i	t	p	z		z	l	h	o
t		c	z	s	u	a	s	e	e	p	l
o		k	e		s		p	s	g	o	i
o	f	l	a	g			o		e	p	v
n	i	n	v	i	t	a	t	i	o	n	e

H Look at the pictures. Find six differences.

JUNE

P. 68

P. 72

JUNE

11

▶

Accompanying audio tracks can be found on Presentation plus or online.

🗨 Let's speak!

Optional extra speaking practice at the back of the Student's Book allows learners to practise the language needed for the speaking part of the Cambridge English: Flyers test.

🔊 ▶ Let's say!

Optional pronunciation practice at the back of the Student's Book focuses on initial key sounds to develop early speaking skills. Supported by accompanying audio.

How could teachers use *Storyfun 5*?

1 Encourage learners to predict the general topic of the story using flashcards and the story pictures.
2 Teach or revise any Cambridge English: Flyers words that are important in the story.
3 Play the audio or read the story.
4 (Optional) Discuss the story 'value' with learners. You will probably need to do this in your learners' first language to fully explore what the story teaches the reader.
5 Present the vocabulary and general comprehension tasks (usually Activities A–C).
6 Present the grammar, vocabulary and skills sections (generally Activities D–H).
7 Encourage collaborative learning with the *Let's have fun!* pages at the back of the Student's Book.
8 Follow communicative pair- or group-work suggestions in the *Let's speak!* pages at the back of the Student's Book.
9 Use extension activities in the Teacher's Books or set homework tasks.

How is the Teacher's Book organised?

Main topics and grammar
Cambridge English: Flyers topics and grammar focused on in the activities in this unit.

Story summary

Main vocabulary
Cambridge English: Flyers vocabulary focused on in the activities in this unit.

Practice for Flyers
Specific activities that gently build up learners' familiarity with the Cambridge English: Flyers test task types.

Equipment
Any equipment or materials needed for teaching the unit, including photocopiables, digital flashcards, audio.

Activity notes
A, B, C, etc. sections correspond to Student's Book activities.

IA Interactive activity
Activity that can also be completed interactively on Presentation plus.

Answer keys
Answers or suggested answers.

Storytelling
Extended notes for approaching storytelling with your learners give detailed suggestions on how to fully exploit digital resources and prompt meaningful and motivating discussions.

Value
The value can be explored and discussed with learners after reading the story. Discussion is optional, either directly after listening or when learners attempt the value activity.

Audioscripts
All scripts for listening activities in the Student's Book. Scripts for stories are not listed.

Extension activities
Flexible ideas to extend activities either in class or for homework.

Test tips and practice
Specific tips for the Cambridge English: Flyers test with optional accompanying activity.

Let's have fun!
Notes for optional projects or games at the back of the Student's Book for each unit.

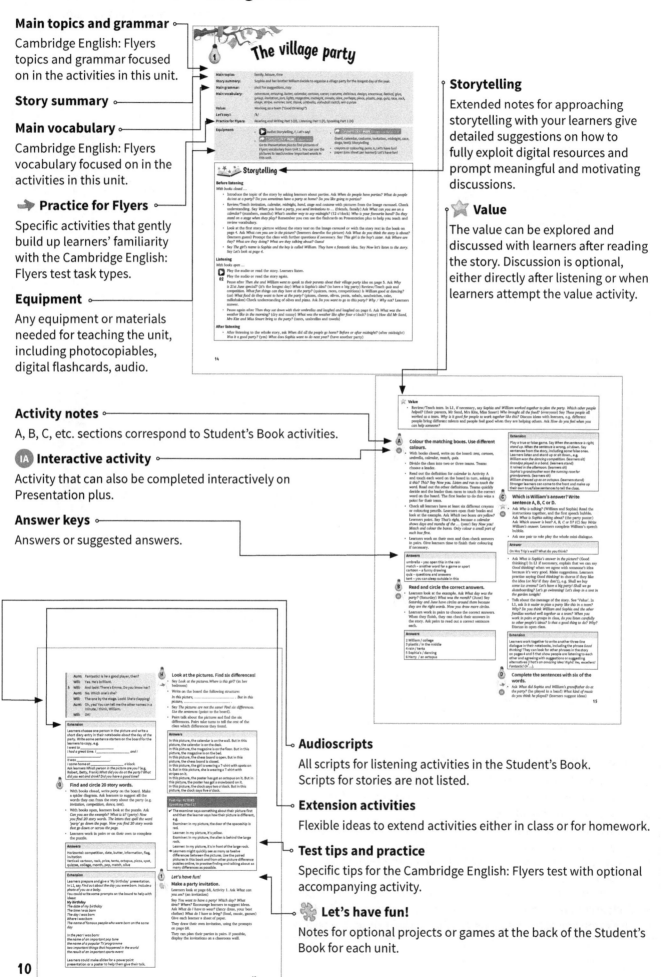

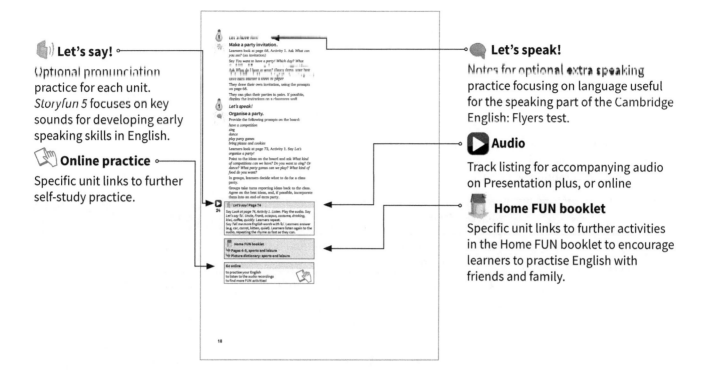

Let's say!

Optional pronunciation practice for each unit. *Storyfun 5* focuses on key sounds for developing early speaking skills in English.

Online practice

Specific unit links to further self-study practice.

Let's speak!

Notes for optional extra speaking practice focusing on language useful for the speaking part of the Cambridge English: Flyers test.

Audio

Track listing for accompanying audio on Presentation plus, or online

Home FUN booklet

Specific unit links to further activities in the Home FUN booklet to encourage learners to practise English with friends and family.

How is the digital organised?

Presentation plus

Interactive activities

Every 'Activity A' in each unit is interactive to check vocabulary comprehension after reading the story and encourage whole-class participation. Other IA activities can be used as a supporting feature, either as a means of introducing an activity, scaffolding, or during answer feedback.

Audio

Audio can be launched from the audio icon. Accompanying audioscripts can be displayed on screen.

Answer key

All activities have a visual answer key to easily display and check answers with your learners.

Digital flashcards

All Cambridge English: Flyers test words are supported with visual flashcards with accompanying audio.

Image carousel

These additional images can be used to prompt further discussion on themes and concepts. Ideas of when and how to use them are within the teacher's notes for each unit.

Each story also has a collection of separate images of the Student's Book pictures without text to prompt discussion before learners open their books and listen, revise the story if heard in a previous lesson or to use as a wrapping-up activity where learners can re-tell the story they've listened to.

Online practice

For the Teacher
o   Presentation plus
o   All audio recordings
o   Additional digital resources to support your classes

For the Student
o   Fun activities to practise the exam, skills and language
o   All audio recordings
o   Additional digital resources

Word FUN World app

Checklist for Cambridge English: Flyers

Storyfun 5 gently introduces learners to Cambridge English: Flyers test-style practice. Activities are carefully graded to ensure learners are guided towards the Flyers level. Full examples of Cambridge English: Flyers test tasks can be found in *Storyfun 6*.

Paper	Part	Task	Unit
Listening 25 minutes	1	Draw lines between names and people in a picture.	Practice: 1, 5
	2	Write words or numbers in a form.	Practice: 4, 6
	3	Match pictures with illustrated words.	Practice: 4, 6
	4	Tick boxes under the correct picture.	Practice: 3, 7
	5	Colour or write in parts of a picture.	Practice: 2, 3, 8
Reading and Writing 40 minutes	1	Copy correct words next to definitions.	Practice: 4, 5, 7, 8
	2	Choose correct responses by circling a letter.	Practice: 6, 8
	3	Choose and copy missing words into a story text.	Practice: 1, 2
	4	Complete a text by copying the correct grammatical words.	Practice: 2, 5, 7
	5	Complete sentences about a story by writing one, two, three or four words.	Practice: 4, 8
	6	Write words in gapped diary/letter. No words are given.	Practice: 5
	7	Write a short story by describing events in three pictures.	Practice: 2, 3
Speaking 7–9 minutes	1	Talk about the differences between two pictures.	Practice: 1, 5, 7
	2	Ask and answer questions about people or objects.	Practice: 4, 8
	3	Tell a story by describing pictures.	Practice: 2, 7
	4	Answer personal questions.	Practice: 2, 4, 7, 8

Map of the Student's Book

Story and Unit	Value	Topics	Grammar	Practice for Flyers
1 The village party	Working as a team (*"Good thinking!"*)	family leisure time	*shall* for suggestions *may*	Reading and Writing Part 3 Listening Part 1 Speaking Part 1
2 Ben's wishes	Being grateful for small things (*"I'm so lucky!"*)	natural world food and drink family	adverbs of frequency: *always, often, sometimes, never, usually* adverbs of place: *anywhere, somewhere, nowhere, everywhere*	Reading and Writing Parts 3, 4 and 7 Listening Part 5 Speaking Parts 3 and 4
3 Treasure	Finding ways to do something difficult (*"Of course I can!"*)	leisure body and face	question tags modals: *might* and *could* *shall* for suggestions	Reading and Writing Part 7 Listening Parts 4 and 5
4 The king's colours	Being patient (*"I can wait. I don't mind."*)	animals colours natural world materials	*make somebody/ something* + adjective *be made of* *Where* clauses	Reading and Writing Parts 1 and 5 Listening Parts 2 and 3 Speaking Parts 2 and 4
5 Robert's envelopes	Hoping to achieve an ambition (*"One day, perhaps!"*)	places and transport	conjunctions: *if, so, after* + clause	Reading and Writing Parts 1, 4 and 6 Listening Part 1 Speaking Part 1
6 Lara and the mountain lion	Helping each other (*"How can I help you now?"*)	health work natural world sports animals	*so* (conjunction and adverb)	Reading and Writing Part 2 Listening Parts 2 and 3
7 Harry's diary	Being forgiving (*"Never mind!"*)	home time	past continuous *still* and *already* *taste, smell, sound, feel, look like* + noun phrase	Reading and Writing Parts 1 and 4 Listening Part 4 Speaking Parts 1, 3 and 4
8 Summer fun	Asking for help when you need it (*"Thanks for your help!"*)	friends jobs	*as … as* *going to*	Reading and Writing Parts 1, 2 and 5 Listening Part 5 Speaking Parts 2 and 4

The village party

1

Main topics:	family, leisure, time
Story summary:	Sophia and her brother William decide to organise a village party for the longest day of the year.
Main grammar:	*shall* for suggestions, *may*
Main vocabulary:	*adventure, amazing, butter, calendar, cartoon, corner, costume, delicious, design, enormous, festival, glue, group, invitation, jam, lights, magazine, midnight, minute, olive, perhaps, piece, plastic, pop, quiz, race, rock, stage, stripe, summer, tent, thank, umbrella, volleyball match, win a prize*
Value:	Working as a team (*"Good thinking!"*)
Let's say!:	/k/
Practice for Flyers:	Reading and Writing Part 3 (D), Listening Part 1 (F), Speaking Part 1 (H)

Equipment:	• ▶ audio: Storytelling, F, Let's say! •  presentation **PLUS** flashcards Go to Presentation plus to find pictures of Flyers vocabulary from Unit 1. You can use the pictures to teach/review important words in this unit.	• ➲ presentation **PLUS** Image carousel 1–8 (band, calendar, costume, invitation, midnight, race, stage, tent): Storytelling • crayons or colouring pencils: A, Let's have fun! • paper (one sheet per learner): Let's have fun!

✦ Storytelling

Before listening

With books closed …

- Introduce the topic of the story by asking learners about parties. Ask *When do people have parties? What do people do/eat at a party? Do you sometimes have a party at home? Do you like going to parties?*
- Review/Teach *invitation, calendar, month, midnight, band, stage* and *costume* with pictures from the Image carousel. Check understanding. Say *When you have a party, you send invitations to …* (my friends, my family) Ask *What can you see on a calendar?* (numbers, months) *What's another way to say midnight?* (12 o'clock) *Who is your favourite band? Do they stand on a stage when they play?* Remember you can use the flashcards on Presentation plus to help you teach and review vocabulary.
- Look at the first story picture without the story text on the Image carousel or with the story text in the book on page 4. Ask *What can you see in the picture?* (learners describe the picture) Ask *What do you think the story is about?* (learners guess) Prompt the class with further questions if necessary. Say *This girl is the boy's sister.* Ask *Where are they? What are they doing? What are they talking about? Guess!*
- Say *The girl's name is Sophia and the boy is called William. They have a fantastic idea.* Say *Now let's listen to the story.* Say *Let's look at page 4.*

Listening

With books open …

Play the audio or read the story. Learners listen.

02 Play the audio or read the story again.

Pause after *Then she and William went to speak to their parents about their village party idea* on page 5. Ask *Why is 21 June special?* (it's the longest day) *What is Sophia's idea?* (to have a big party) Review/Teach *quiz* and *competition.* Ask *What fun things can they have at the party?* (quizzes, races, competitions) *Is William good at dancing?* (no) *What food do they want to have at the party?* (pizzas, cheese, olives, pasta, salads, sandwiches, cake, milkshakes) Check understanding of *olives* and *pizza.* Ask *Do you want to go to this party? Why? / Why not?* Learners answer.

- Pause again after *Then they sat down with their umbrellas and laughed and laughed* on page 6. Ask *What was the weather like in the morning?* (dry and sunny) *What was the weather like after four o'clock?* (rainy) *What did Mr Sand, Mrs Kite and Miss Smart bring to the party?* (tents, umbrellas and towels)

After listening

- After listening to the whole story, ask *When did all the people go home? Before or after midnight?* (after midnight) *Was it a good party?* (yes) *What does Sophia want to do next year?* (have another party)

A Colour the matching boxes. Use different colours.

- With books closed, write on the board: *tent, cartoon, umbrella, calendar, match, quiz.*

- Divide the class into two or three teams. Teams choose a leader.

- Read out the definition for *calendar* in Activity A and touch each word on the board in turn, asking *Is it this? This?* Say *Now you! Listen and run to touch the word.* Read out the other definitions. Teams quickly decide and the leader then races to touch the correct word on the board. The first leader to do this wins a point for their team.

- Check all learners have at least six different crayons or colouring pencils. Learners open their books and look at the example. Ask *Which two boxes are yellow?* Learners point. Say *That's right, because a calendar shows days and months of the …* (year) Say *Now you! Match and colour the boxes. Only colour a small part of each box first.*

- Learners work on their own and then check answers in pairs. Give learners time to finish their colouring if necessary.

Answers

umbrella – you open this in the rain
match – another word for a game or sport
cartoon – a funny drawing
quiz – questions and answers
tent – you can sleep outside in this

B Read and circle the correct answer.

- Learners look at the example. Ask *What day was the party?* (Saturday) *What was the month?* (June) Say *'Saturday' and 'June' have circles around them because they are the right words. Now you draw more circles.*

- Learners work in pairs to choose the correct answers. When they finish, they can check their answers in the story. Ask pairs to read out a correct sentence each.

Answers

2 William / college
3 plastic / in the middle
4 rain / tents
5 Sophia's / dancing
6 Harry / an octopus

Extension

Play a true or false game. Say *When the sentence is right, stand up. When the sentence is wrong, sit down.* Say sentences from the story, including some false ones. Learners listen and stand up or sit down, e.g.
William won the dancing competition. (learners sit)
Grandpa played in a band. (learners stand)
It rained in the afternoon. (learners stand)
Sophia's grandmother won the running race for grandparents. (learners stand)
William dressed up as an octopus. (learners sit)
Stronger learners can come to the front of the class and say their own true or false sentences about the story. The class stand up or sit down as before.

C Which is William's answer? Write sentence A, B, C or D.

- Ask *Who is talking?* (William and Sophia) Read the instructions together, and the first speech bubble. Ask *What is Sophia asking about?* (the party poster) Ask *Which answer is best? A, B, C or D?* (C) Say *Write William's answer.* Learners complete William's speech bubble.

- Ask one pair to role play the whole mini-dialogue.

Answer

On Mrs Trip's wall? What do you think?

- Ask *What is Sophia's answer in the picture?* (Yes. Good thinking!) In L1 if necessary, explain that we can say *Good thinking!* when we agree with someone's idea because it's very good. Make suggestions. Learners practise saying *Good thinking!* in chorus if they like the idea (or *No!* if they don't), e.g. *Shall we buy some ice creams! Let's have a big party! Shall we go skateboarding? Let's go swimming! Let's sleep in a tent in the garden tonight!*

- Talk about the message of the story. See 'Value' above. In L1, ask *Is it easier to plan a party like this in a team? Why? Do you think William and Sophia and the other families worked well together as a team? When you work in pairs or groups in class, do you listen carefully to other people's ideas? Is that a good thing to do? Why?* Discuss in open class.

Extension

Learners work together to write another three-line dialogue in their notebooks, including the phrase *Good thinking!* They can look for other phrases in the story on pages 4 and 5 that show people are listening to each other and agreeing with suggestions or suggesting alternatives (*That's an amazing idea! Right! Yes, excellent! Fantastic! Or …*).

Complete the sentences with six of the words.

- Ask *What did Sophia and William's grandfather do at the party?* (he played in a band) *What kind of music do you think he played?* (learners suggest ideas)

- Review/Teach words for *talk*. Ask *How can we say 'talk' in another way?* Learners suggest words they know, e.g. *ask, answer, call, chat, say, speak, tell, thank, whisper.* Make a list on the board.

- Read out the instruction and the first two sentences, including the example. Ask *Who are the people in the band?* (Grandfather, Richard and Fred) Ask *Why is 'called' crossed out in the box?* (because it's the answer to number 1) Ask *How many more gaps are there?* (five) *How many more words are in the box?* (eight) *Do you need to use all the words in the box?* (no) *Now you read and complete the text.*

- Learners work on their own and then compare answers with a partner. Learners read out complete sentences to check their answers.

- Say *Now choose the best name for this story and tick the box.* In pairs, learners choose the title.

Answers

2 tunes **3** chat **4** heard **5** grandson **6** weeks
The band play at the party.

- Ask *Do you think Grandfather's band plays good music? Do you play in a band? Would you like to be in a band one day? Can you play the guitar? The drums? The piano? The violin?*

Test tip: FLYERS
Reading and Writing (Part 3)

- ✔ Learners complete a story text by choosing five words (not including the example) from a possible ten. These might be nouns, verbs, adverbs or adjectives.
- ➜ Practise completing sentences with adjectives and adverbs after *very* and *really*. Write on the board, e.g. *That boy is really _____ . That boy runs really _____ .* Pairs choose their own adjectives and adverbs to complete the sentences.
  Practise completing sentences with the correct verb form. Write on the board, e.g. *I _____ skateboarding every Monday after school. I _____ skateboarding yesterday. I haven't _____ skateboarding since last summer.* Learners complete the sentences with the correct form of the verb.

Talk with a friend about the weekend. Say *may* or *may not*.

- Review/Teach *usually, perhaps* and *maybe*. Explain that *perhaps* and *maybe* mean the same.

- With books closed, ask *What do you usually do at the weekend?* Learners suggest ideas (e.g. *I usually go shopping. I usually play sport. I always visit my grandparents.*) Say *Next weekend I may go to the cinema.*

- Write the sentence on the board, underlining *may*. Ask *Am I going to the cinema? Yes, no or maybe?* (maybe) Say *Think about what you may do.*

- Learners open their books and read the example. Ask *Does the boy want to go to the park at the weekend?* (perhaps/maybe) *Why?* (because he wants to fly his kite)

- In pairs, learners talk about what they may do, using the prompts.

- Feed back in open class, asking, e.g. *Who may watch a movie? Who may go swimming?*

Listen and draw lines.

- Learners look at the picture. Ask *What can you see?* Learners describe the picture. If necessary, prompt learners with questions: *How many people can you see? What is the girl who is sitting on the cushion wearing? What is the boy with brown hair on the stage doing?*

- Say *William is talking to his aunt about the village party.* Learners look at the example. Say *Listen and draw lines from the people in the picture to their names. You don't need to use all the names.*

03

- Play the audio. Pause after the example and ask *Which boy is Robert?* (learners point to the boy with the sandwich and milkshake)

- Play the rest of the audio. Learners draw lines and then compare their answers. Listen a second time if needed. Check answers in open class. Ask, e.g. *What's Frank doing? What's Emma wearing?*

Answers

Betty – girl on red cushion with tablet
Holly – girl with hands in the air
George – boy on yellow chair drawing cartoons
Frank – boy playing guitar
Emma – girl by stage, clapping

Tapescript:

Will:	Look, here's a picture of the party. We had it in our street!
Aunt:	Wow! What a lot of people! Who's that? The person with the milkshake and sandwich?
Will:	That's Robert. He's one of my friends at college. We're in the same group.
Aunt:	Oh!

Can you see the line? This is an example.
Now you listen and draw lines.

1	**Aunt:**	Oh! Is that one of your friends as well? The girl sitting on that red cushion?
	Will:	Yes. She's called Betty. She wanted to chat with someone who couldn't come to the party.
	Aunt:	But she isn't using her phone …
	Will:	No, but you can do that with a tablet too.
2	**Will:**	… and there's Holly!
	Aunt:	Where?
	Will:	She's the girl with her hands up in the air.
	Aunt:	Oh – the girl in the middle.
	Will:	Yes.
3	**Aunt:**	That person there looks too young to be a friend of yours. Is he one of Sophia's classmates?
	Will:	The boy on the yellow chair? The one who's drawing cartoons? Yes.
	Aunt:	What's his name?
	Will:	George, I think … Yes, that's right. He preferred doing that. He doesn't like dancing.

4	**Aunt:**	And is that instrument a guitar? It doesn't look like yours.
	Will:	Oh, you mean Frank's? Yes, it is! He loves playing rock music! He may enter a music competition next month.
	Aunt:	Fantastic! Is he a good player, then?
	Will:	Yes. He's brilliant.
5	**Will:**	And look! There's Emma. Do you know her?
	Aunt:	No. Which one's she?
	Will:	The one by the stage. Look! She's clapping!
	Aunt:	Oh, yes! You can tell me the other names in a minute, I think, William.
	Will:	OK!

Extension

Learners choose one person in the picture and write a short diary entry in their notebooks about the day of the party. Write some sentence starters on the board for the learners to copy, e.g.

I went to _____ .
I had a great time. I _____ and I
_____ .
It was _____ .
I came home at _____ o'clock.
Ask learners *Which person in the picture are you?* (e.g. Robert, Betty, Frank) *What did you do at the party? What did you eat and drink? Did you have a good time?*

G   Find and circle 20 story words.

- With books closed, write *party* on the board. Make a spider diagram. Ask learners to suggest all the words they can from the story about the party (e.g. *invitation, competition, dance, tent*).

- With books open, learners look at the puzzle. Ask *Can you see the example? What is it?* (party) Say *The letters that spell the word 'party' go down the page. Now you find 19 more story words that go down or across the page.*

- Learners work in pairs or on their own to complete the puzzle.

Answers

Horizontal: competition, date, butter, information, flag, invitation
Vertical: cartoon, rock, prize, tents, octopus, pizza, spot, quizzes, college, month, pop, match, olive

Extension

Learners prepare and give a 'My birthday' presentation. In L1, say *Find out about the day you were born. Include a photo of you as a baby.*
You could write some prompts on the board to help with ideas:
My birthday
The date of my birthday
The time I was born
The day I was born
Where I was born
The name of famous people who were born on the same day

In the year I was born:
the name of an important pop tune
the name of a popular TV programme
two important things that happened in the world
the result of an important sports event

Learners could make slides for a presentation or a poster to help them give their talk.

H   Look at the pictures. Find six differences.

- Say *Look at the pictures. Where is this girl?* (in her bedroom)

- Write on the board the following structure:
  In this picture, ... But in this picture, ...

- Say *The pictures are not the same! Find six differences. Use the sentences* (point to the board).

- Pairs talk about the pictures and find the six differences. Pairs take turns to tell the rest of the class which differences they found.

Answers

In this picture, the calendar is on the wall. But in this picture, the calendar is on the desk.
In this picture, the magazine is on the floor. But in this picture, the magazine is on the bed.
In this picture, the chess board is open. But in this picture, the chess board is closed.
In this picture, the girl is wearing a T-shirt with spots on it. But in this picture, she is wearing a T-shirt with stripes on it.
In this picture, the poster has got an octopus on it. But in this picture, the poster has got a snowboard on it.
In this picture, the clock says two o'clock. But in this picture, the clock says five o'clock.

Test tip: FLYERS
Speaking (Part 1)

✔ The examiner says something about their picture first and then the learner says how their picture is different, e.g.
  Examiner: In my picture, the door of the spaceship is red.
  Learner: In my picture, it's yellow.
  Examiner: In my picture, the alien is behind the large rock.
  Learner: In my picture, it's in front of the large rock.

➜ Learners might quickly see as many as 12 differences between the pictures. Use the paired pictures in this book, and from other picture difference puzzles online, to practise finding and talking about as many differences as possible.

Let's have fun!

Make a party invitation.

Learners look at page 68, Activity 1. Ask *What can you see?* (an invitation)

Say *You want to have a party! Which day? What time? Where?* Encourage learners to suggest ideas. Ask *What do I have to wear?* (fancy dress, your best clothes) *What do I have to bring?* (food, music, games) Give each learner a sheet of paper.

They draw their own invitation, using the prompts on page 68.

They can plan their parties in pairs. If possible, display the invitations on a classroom wall.

Let's speak!

Organise a party.

Provide the following prompts on the board:

have a competition
sing
dance
play party games
bring pizzas and cookies

Learners look at page 72, Activity 1. Say *Let's organise a party!*

Point to the ideas on the board and ask *What kind of competitions can we have? Do you want to sing? Or dance? What party games can we play? What kind of food do you want?*

In groups, learners decide what to do for a class party.

Groups take turns reporting ideas back to the class. Agree on the best ideas, and, if possible, incorporate them into an end-of-term party.

24

Let's say! Page 74

Say *Look at page 74, Activity 1. Listen.* Play the audio. Say *Let's say* /k/. *Uncle, Frank, octopus, costume, drinking, kiwi, coffee, quickly.* Learners repeat.
Say *Tell me more English words with* /k/. Learners answer (e.g. car, carrot, kitten, quiet). Learners listen again to the audio, repeating the rhyme as fast as they can.

Home FUN booklet

➡ **Pages 4–5, sports and leisure**
➡ **Picture dictionary: sports and leisure**

Go online

to practise your English
to listen to the audio recordings
to find more FUN activities!

Ben's wishes

2

Main topics:	natural world, food and drink, family
Story summary:	Ben wants to learn about the world, but he has to work in the fields every day. One day he finds a magic cup.
Main grammar:	adverbs of frequency: *always, often, sometimes, never, usually,* adverbs of place: *anywhere, somewhere, nowhere, everywhere*
Main vocabulary:	*creature, delicious, early, Earth, interesting, land, ocean, pleased, rucksack, silver, still, through, unkind, wonderful*
Value:	Being grateful for small things (*"I'm so lucky!"*)
Let's say!:	/ʌ/
Practice for Flyers:	Reading and Writing Part 3 (A), Listening Part 5 (D), Reading and Writing Part 7 (G), Speaking Part 3 (G), Reading and Writing Part 4 (H), Speaking Part 4 (Let's speak!)

Equipment:	• ▶ audio: Storytelling, D, Let's say! • ⮕ (presentation **PLUS**) flashcards Go to Presentation plus to find pictures of Flyers vocabulary from Unit 2. You can use the pictures to teach/review important words in this unit. • ⮕ (presentation **PLUS**) Image carousel 9–13 (dig, fight, hole, lucky, gorilla): Storytelling, G, H	• Photocopy 2, one per learner (TB page 54): Storytelling Extension • crayons or colouring pencils: Storytelling Extension, D, H, Let's have fun! • a coat, a cup, two bowls, two spoons, ten books (optional): E Extension • paper (one sheet per learner): Let's have fun!

 **Storytelling**

Before listening

With books closed …

- Introduce the topic of the story by asking learners about wishes. Say *What would you really like to have? What would you really like to do?* Learners' answers should begin with *I'd like to,* e.g. *I'd like to go to Africa. I'd like to be a footballer. I'd like to have lots of books.* Write the ideas on the board.
- Say *This story is about a boy called Ben and about his wishes. Ben lives with his two brothers on a small farm.*
- Look at the first story picture without the story text on the Image carousel or with the story text in the book on page 12.
- Ask *Are these three boys brothers? Which boy is Ben?* (learners guess) Review/Teach *money, rich* and *poor.* Show some money and ask *Do these boys have lots of money or no money? Are they rich or poor?* Learners answer.
- Review/Teach *hole, lucky, dig* and *fight* using the pictures on the Image carousel. Check understanding, saying *We say someone is lucky when something really great happens to them.* Ask *Which people are lucky?* (people who win competitions, get lovely birthday presents, aren't ill / have kind friends / live in happy families)
- Mime *dig* and *fight* and show the pictures on the Image carousel. Ask *What can people dig a hole in?* (the ground, a road) Ask *Do you have brothers or sisters who fight sometimes?*
- Remember you can use the flashcards on Presentation plus to help you teach and review vocabulary.
- Say *Now let's listen to the story.* Say *Let's look at page 12.*

Listening

With books open …

 04

- Play the audio or read the story. Learners listen.
- Play the audio or read the story again.
- Pause after *he put it down on the grass next to his rucksack* on page 13. Ask *What did the older boys want Ben to do that day?* (dig up vegetables, make soup) *Were the older boys horrible to Ben?* (yes) *Where did Ben work that day?* (in the fields) *What did Ben find there?* (an old silver cup)
- Pause again after *sat down by the fire and read them all* on page 14. Ask *What's Ben doing now?* (reading his new books) *Has he made the soup for dinner?* (no) *Will his brothers be angry?* (yes)

After listening

- After listening to the whole story, ask *Was the cup OK at the end of the story?* (no) Mime *breaking* and say *The cup …* (broke) *How did you feel when the cup broke? Were you happy?* (learners respond)

Value

- Say *In the story, Ben's first wish was just for a warm drink. He didn't want lots of money. And he felt very lucky when he got that.*
- Review/Teach *grateful* and then, in L1, discuss the importance of being grateful for our basic things. Ask *Do possessions like expensive clothes make you happy? What makes you happy that costs nothing? Is it important to remember that sometimes a walk in a nice place in nice weather with fun friends or our family can make us happier than having a new sweater or computer game? Many poor people are happier than many rich people in the world. Do you agree or disagree with that? What do you feel grateful for?* Learners answer in English or L1.

Extension: Photocopy 2

Give each learner Photocopy 2 (TB page 54). Say *Each square is one day of the week.*

Learners decide how many squares to colour in to show how many days in one week *never, sometimes, usually, often, always* might look like. Learners can colour half boxes if they like. If learners are not sure, tell them how many squares to colour in each row, e.g.

never: no squares coloured
sometimes: one or two squares coloured
often: three or four squares coloured
usually: five or six squares coloured
always: seven squares coloured

Ask *What did Ben never/always do?* Learners suggest their own ideas, e.g. *Ben never went to school. Ben always worked in the fields.*

Learners look at the five questions. They take turns to ask you these questions first. Answer with your own ideas or invent answers, e.g. *I never eat crocodile meat. I sometimes drink pineapple juice. I often talk to my uncle. I usually sit on my sofa at home. I always clean my teeth at night.*

In pairs, learners ask and answer the same questions. Ask four or five learners to tell the class one of their own or one of their partner's answers.

A Complete each answer with one of the words.

- Learners look at the example. Ask *What has got a hole in it?* (the sock) Say *Now you! Use these words to complete the sentences. How many more words do you need?* (five) Learners work on their own and then check answers in pairs.

Answers

2 money **3** winter **4** ocean **5** creature **6** Earth

Extension

In their notebooks, pairs write questions with answers that include the unused words (*minute* and *fire*), e.g,
When does the film start? In one minute.
Are you cold? Yes. Let's make a fire.

B Read and tick (✔) the correct box.

- Learners look at Activity B. Ask *What do you have to do?* (tick the 'Right' or 'Wrong' box)
- Learners look at the example and at the ticked 'Wrong' box. Ask *Which word is wrong?* (summer) Say *Yes, the girl heard the story in the … (winter)*
- In pairs, learners tick the correct box for sentences 2–6. You can make this a race.
- Check answers in open class. Ask learners to correct the 'wrong' sentences. They can look at the story to find the right answers.

Answers

2 Right **3** Wrong **4** Wrong **5** Wrong **6** Right

- Say *We make the opposites of some words by adding 'un-' at the beginning of the word.* Ask *What's the opposite of 'kind'? Look in the story.* (unkind) Say *In the story, the brothers are 'unkind'.* Write *unkind* on the board. Say *Do you know more words beginning with 'un-'?* (learners suggest ideas) Flyers adjectives that begin with un- are: *unfriendly, unhappy, unkind, untidy* and *unusual.* Write these words on the board and ask *What's the opposite of 'untidy'? What's the opposite of 'unhappy'?* etc.

Extension

In pairs, learners write three more sentences about the story. Say *One of your sentences should be wrong.* Pairs write sentences and then swap sentences with another pair. Say *Tick the right sentences and make the wrong sentence correct.* Walk around and help if necessary.

C Who is talking about the story? Tick (✔) A, B or C.

- Say *These girls are talking about three different stories. Only one of them read 'Ben's wishes'. Was it A, B or C?*
- Learners read the speech bubbles and underline important words, e.g. A *lazy*, B *lucky* and C *kind*. In pairs, learners look at the important words and choose their answer.
- Ask *Was it A? Was it B? Was it C?* Learners put up their hands to vote on which answer they think is right.
- Learners say why A and C aren't right, e.g. *A – Ben wasn't lazy. He worked hard in the fields. He wanted to go to school. C – Ben's brothers were unkind. They didn't help him.*

Answer

B

- Talk about the message of the story. See 'Value' above.
- Say *Let's talk more about Ben now. He says he's lucky, but he doesn't have many things.*
- Teach *I'm so lucky.* Say *'So' here means the same as 'very' or 'really'.*
- Ask *Is Ben a good person? Why?*

D Look at the picture on page 12. Listen, colour and write.

- Learners look carefully at the picture on page 12 again. In pairs, they find things that begin with the letter *f*. Give them two minutes to do this. Ask *Has anyone got more than five? Six? Seven? Eight?*

- Pairs suggest one word each. Other pairs can put their hands up to show they found the same word. Write all their suggestions on the board. Accept any reasonable answers.

Suggested answers

face, family, field, floor, fire, foot, feet, fork, frog

- Say *Now listen to a girl and her teacher. Listen carefully. Think about what you should colour, what you should draw and where you should draw it.*

- Check that each learner has crayons or colouring pencils.

05

- Play the audio twice. Give learners time to finish their colouring and to show each other their pictures.

- Check answers, asking *What's red?* (the fire) *What's yellow?* (the plates) *What's green?* (the leaf) *Which word did you write?* (onions) *Where did you write your word?* (on the box)

Answers

fire – red
plates – yellow
leaf – green
'Onions' written on the box under the window

Tapescript:

Girl:	This picture needs some colour! Can I do some colouring here?
Man:	Yes! Of course you can. Can you see the scarf?
Girl:	You mean the one by the door? Yes! Can I colour it blue?
Man:	Yes, please. Do that now.
Girl:	OK.

Can you see the blue scarf? This is an example. Now you listen and colour and write.

1	**Man:**	Now colour the fire. It's behind Ben.
	Girl:	Oh, yes! What colour shall I make it? Orange?
	Man:	No. Fires sometimes look red … Let's make it red instead, please.
	Girl:	No problem! There!

2	**Girl:**	Can I write something in this picture too?
	Man:	Yes. There's a box under the window. Write 'onions' on that.
	Girl:	Oh. OK. Is that where Ben puts the onions he gets from the fields?
	Man:	Yes. He usually puts them there.
3	**Man:**	Now colour the three plates. They're empty here, of course.
	Girl:	Yes! Which colour shall I use for those?
	Man:	Make them yellow. Have you got that colour?
	Girl:	Sure! Here! I'm colouring those now.
	Man:	Great!
4	**Girl:**	Can I colour the leaf? There's only one. It's on the ground behind the brothers.
	Man:	Yes, you can colour that as well.
	Girl:	Fantastic! Can I colour it green?
	Man:	Yes.
	Girl:	Thank you. I like this picture more now.
	Man:	So do I!

Test tip: FLYERS
Listening (Part 5)

✔ Learners listen to a conversation about a picture. They will need to colour parts of the picture and also add two words. The words are usually common or proper nouns (names). Learners need to write the word in the correct place and to spell the word correctly. Sometimes the word they should write goes before or after a word that is already in the picture.

→ Learners could practise following instructions to write common or proper nouns before or after given words. For example, if you have read a text about a city, say *Draw a signpost in your notebook. Write 'To the' on your signpost. Now write 'city' after 'To the'.* If you have read a text about a hotel, say *Let's write the name of that hotel. Write 'Hotel' in your notebooks now. Before the word 'Hotel' write 'Spruce'. You spell that S-P-R-U-C-E. It's called Spruce Hotel.*

In pairs, learners could choose proper nouns and give spelling instructions for their partner to follow.

E Choose the best answer. Write a letter (A–H).

- Learners look at the two small faces in the conversation. Ask *Who are these?* (Paul and Ben) Ask *Who is Paul?* (Ben's brother)

- Look at the example together. Ask *Why is the answer B?* (the other sentences aren't an answer for this question) Ask a pair to read out the conversation.

- Say *Look! Sentence B has a line through it now.* Ask *How many other answers must we choose?* (five) *How many other answers are there?* (seven) Say *You don't need two of these answers.*

- In pairs, learners then complete 2–6 by choosing the best answer from the A–H options.

- Check answers in open class.

Answers

2 G   3 E   4 A   5 H   6 C

- Divide the class into A and B teams. Tell team A they are Paul. Tell team B they are Ben. Teams then read out their lines to complete the conversation.

F Find and write the words.

- Explain these adverbs of place and their examples, in L1 if necessary:

We use 'anywhere' in questions and negative statements. It means 'in any place' or 'to any place'. For example, 'Have you seen my new coat anywhere?' 'I don't want to go anywhere.'

We use 'everywhere' to mean 'in every place' or 'to every place'. For example, 'I've looked for my books everywhere!' 'I've been everywhere in the world.'

We use 'somewhere' to mean 'in a place' (but we don't know where) or 'to a place' (but we don't know where). For example, 'My money is here somewhere. Can you help me find it?' 'My friend and I want to go out somewhere today – perhaps to the beach.'

We use 'nowhere' to mean 'in no place'. We can only use it at this level in positive statements in this simple structure: 'I can't find my school bag. It's nowhere in the house.'

- Learners look at the word snake and work on their own to find and circle the four words. They check their answers with a partner. Then check answers in open class.

- Say *Now complete each sentence with one of the words.* In pairs, learners choose and write the correct word for each sentence.

Answers

1 somewhere **2** everywhere **3** nowhere **4** anywhere

- Ask *Which sentence is about the picture? (3) Where's the money now? What do you think?* (learners guess)

G What did Ben do next? Look and write. Then tell the story.

- Use the Image carousel picture to teach *gorilla*.

- Learners look at the pictures in Activity G. Ask *What can you see here?* Write learners' key word suggestions on the board, e.g. *map, school, teacher, bed, books, train, bags, station, platform, jungle, plants, notebook, rucksack, gorilla.*

- Divide learners into groups of three or four. Learners look at the pictures and read the prompts. They complete the sentences with one, two, three, four or five words to write a short story about what Ben did after the cup broke.

- Give learners plenty of time to complete the task. Walk around and help where necessary.

- Groups take it in turns to read out their stories. The class votes for the best story.

Suggested answers

Ben began going to school. He learnt about other countries in the world. Ben had lots of books. He studied hard in the evening. When Ben was 18, he travelled to Africa on a train. Ben found a gorilla there and then wrote a story.

Test tip: FLYERS
Reading and Writing (Part 7)

- ✔ Learners write a short story about what is happening in a series of three pictures. There is no limit to the number of words in their story, but learners should definitely write more than 20 words.
- → Using any picture in the book, encourage learners to imagine something that happened before and after the scene and then think of different ways to complete a short story. They could do this in small groups or pairs.

H Look and read. Choose the words.

- With books closed, show learners the Image carousel picture of the gorilla again. Ask *What do you know about gorillas?* Accept all valid answers, writing ideas on the board, e.g. *Gorillas live in Africa. They live in forests and in the mountains. They are larger than monkeys.*

- Write these questions on the board:

  a) What name do we use for father gorillas?

  b) What do mountain gorillas like eating?

  c) How many mountain gorillas live in the world?

- Learners read the text to find the answers to the questions: a) Silverbacks b) fruit, leaves, flowers, insects c) 700.

- Say *Look at the example. 'About' is the right word for number 1.* Learners read the text again. Say *Write the correct word in each gap.* You may prefer to do this in open class.

Answers

2 get **3** called **4** changes **5** usually **6** and **7** in **8** them

- Revise time adverbs (*always, often, sometimes, never* and *usually*). Learners circle *sometimes* and *usually* in the text. Write three speech bubbles on the board:

  Before school I often _____ .

  I sometimes _____ .

  I usually _____ .

- Ask learners to complete the sentences about themselves, and then talk about them in pairs.

I Write a verse about you.

- Ask two learners to read aloud the first two verses of the poem for the class. Ask *Which words sound the same?* (coat/goat/boat and hat/bat/cat)

- Ask *What do you wish for?* Learners answer. Write some of their wishes on the board.

- Say *Now you! Write about your wishes.* In pairs, learners help each other complete a third verse. Strong learners can try to choose words with endings which rhyme (e.g. *shoe/zoo/glue* or *whale/snail/ email*). Walk around and help with ideas if necessary. Encourage learners to use dictionaries.

- Learners read their own verses for the class.

2 *Let's have fun!*

Design a book cover.

Learners look at page 68, Activity 2. Ask *What do you have to design?* (a book cover)

Learners read the prompts and plan their answers in their notebooks. Ask a few learners *What's the name of your book? What is the book about?*

Give each learner a sheet of paper. Learners design and create their book cover.

If possible, display the completed book covers on a classroom wall.

2 *Let's speak!*

Ask and answer the questions.

Ask *Where did Ben live?* (on a farm / in an old house) *How old was Ben?* (learners guess) *Ben loved books! What did he like doing?* (reading)

Provide the following prompts on the board:
Brothers / sisters?
Where / live?
Age?
What / like doing?

Learners look at page 72, Activity 2 and read the conversation.

Learners look at the question prompts and ask and answer in pairs about their brothers and sisters or about themselves.

If learners need more support, write the completed questions, with learners' help, on the board:
Have you got any brothers or sisters?
Where do you live?
How old are you?
What do you like doing?

◄)) Let's say! Page 74

25 Say *Look at page 74, Activity 2. Listen.* Play the audio. Say *Let's say /ʌ/. Monday, brothers, hundreds, onions, rucksack, butter, gloves.* Learners repeat.
Say *Tell me more English words with /ʌ/.* Learners answer (e.g. Sunday, honey, hungry, up, umbrella, unkind). Learners listen again to the audio, repeating the rhyme as fast as they can.

 Home FUN booklet

➡ **Pages 6–7, the world around us**
➡ **Picture dictionary: the world around us, food and drink**

Go online

to practise your English
to listen to the audio recordings
to find more FUN activities!

 Treasure

3

Main topics:	leisure, body and face
Story summary:	Emma is bored. A little boy helps her find treasure.
Main grammar:	question tags, modals: *might* and *could*, *shall* for suggestions
Main vocabulary:	*begin, believe, disappear, elbow, explore, finger, fork, frightening, glove, instead, knee, large, middle, problem, pull, quite, store, sunglasses, toe, unusual*
Value:	Finding ways to do something difficult (*"Of course I can!"*)
Let's say!:	/s/
Practice for Flyers:	Listening Part 5 (E), Reading and Writing Part 7 (F), Listening Part 4 (G)

Equipment:	• audio: Storytelling, E, G, I, Let's say!	• Photocopy 3 (TB pages 55–56), cut into cards, and one complete sheet, per group of four to five learners: B Extension
	• ➡ (presentation **PLUS**) flashcards Go to Presentation plus to find pictures of Flyers vocabulary from Unit 3. You can use the pictures to teach/review important words in this unit.	• a towel, sun cream, a hat, swimming goggles, a shell, some stones: C Extension (optional) • toy fishing rod, skipping rope: G (optional) • crayons or colouring pencils: E, Let's have fun!
	• ➡ (presentation **PLUS**) Image carousel 14–18 (bite, crab, deep, finger, hook): Storytelling	• paper (one sheet per learner): Let's have fun!

Storytelling

Before listening

With books closed …

- Introduce the topic of the story. Ask *Do you like going to the beach? What do you like doing on the beach? Which other places do you like going to on holiday?* Review/Teach *hotel*. Say *This story is about a girl who is on holiday. Her hotel is near a beach.*
- Review/Teach *deep, crab, bite, finger* and *hook*, using photographs from the Image carousel. Ask *Where do crabs live?* (in the sea) *How many legs has a crab got?* (eight) *What do we bite with?* (our teeth) *Which is deeper? Water in a river or water in the ocean?* (in the ocean) *How many fingers have we got?* (eight) Remember you can use the flashcards on Presentation plus to help you teach and review vocabulary.
- Look at the first story picture without the story text on the Image carousel or with the story text in the book on page 20. Ask *Where is the girl?* (on the beach) *Is she happy?* (no) *Why?* (learners guess) *How many other people can you see?* (four)
- Say *Now let's listen to the story.* Say *Let's look at page 20.*

Listening

With books open …

 Play the audio or read the story. Learners listen.

06 Play the audio or read the story again.

Pause after *'Shall we begin looking there?' he whispered* on page 21. Ask *Did Emma want to speak to the boy?* (no) *What does the boy want to look for?* (treasure) *What is the boy's father?* (a pirate) *Does Emma look for treasure with the boy?* (yes)

- Pause after *'Let's go back instead'* on page 22. Ask *What did they find in the first rock pool?* (a glove) *And in the second rock pool?* (a fork) *Were the sunglasses that they found old or new?* (old) *Do the girl and the pirate's son go back to the beach?* (learners guess)

After listening

- After listening to the whole story, ask *What's the very best kind of treasure?* (a ring) *Whose ring is it?* (Emma's mum's) *Does Emma think pirates are only in stories now?* (no)

☆ Value

- In L1 if necessary, say *In the story, the pirate's son found a way to do something very difficult.* Ask *What kind of person is the boy?* Accept answers in English and L1, e.g. *helpful, kind, funny, curious, clever, creative.* Discuss problem-solving with learners. Ask *Do you know someone who is helpful and good at solving problems? How have they helped you? Is it important to thank people who help you? How do you feel when you help a friend who has problems? Does it feel good if they thank you for helping them?* Accept answers in English or L1.

A Read and draw lines.

- Ask *What can you see in the picture?* Learners describe the picture in pairs, e.g. *A boy is fishing. He is in a green boat. There are three fish in the sea. A girl is swimming under the water. The big red fish has lots of teeth! There is an orange crab.*

- Learners look at the example. Ask *What colour is the fish next to the girl's fingers?* (red) Say *Now you! Draw lines from the words to the correct parts of the picture.* Walk around and check learners are doing this correctly.

B Put the sentences in order. Write numbers 2–7.

- Learners read the seven sentences on their own. They underline any words that they don't know and then ask you or their partner for help with understanding.

- Say *Find the star with number 1 in it. This was the first thing that happened in the story. What's next?*

- In pairs, learners write numbers 2–7 in the other stars.

- Check answers in open class. A pair reads out sentence 2. Ask the others if they agree or disagree. Continue with the other answers in the same way.

Answers

2, 4, 7, (1), 5, 3, 6

Extension: Photocopy 3

Divide learners into groups of four or five. Give each group a cut-up set of 24 feelings cards from Photocopy 3 (TB pages 55–56). Also give one complete version of Photocopy 3 to each group.
In groups, learners look at the complete photocopy. Ask *How do these people look?* Point to each face and write their suggestions on the board, e.g. *sad/unhappy, bored, angry, afraid, happy, surprised, hot, excited, friendly, cold, ill, tired.*
In their groups, learners each choose a card from their cut-up set. They take turns to show it and say *Today I'm feeling (sad/bored).* They could add a reason, e.g. *... because my best friend isn't here / this isn't interesting.*
Learners might choose a card because it really shows how they are feeling, or simply because they like it.
Stronger groups might follow this with a suggestion, e.g. *Oh! Well, you could play with us. / Well, let's go for a walk. / We can help you. / That's great. Let's go for a swim in the sea!*
Learners replace the cards, choose different ones and play again.

C What kind of person is he? Circle the words.

- Review/Teach *unfriendly.* Write on the board *friendly, tidy, happy* and *usual.* Say *We can add 'un-' to the front of these words to make them mean the opposite.* Ask one learner *Is your best friend friendly or unfriendly? Is the pirate's son friendly or unfriendly?*

- Learners read the speech bubble. Say *Find the part of the story where one person said this.* Learners find and underline *Of course I can!* on page 22. Ask *Who said this?* (the pirate's son) Say *When Emma wanted the pirate's son to do something difficult, he said 'Of course ...'* (I can) Ask *What kind of person is he?*

- Review/Teach the other adjectives if necessary. In pairs, learners choose adjectives to describe the pirate's son, and circle them. Check answers in open class.

Suggested answers

brave, kind, clever, lucky

- Talk about the message of the story. See 'Value' on page 24.

Extension

Bring some beach things into class, e.g. a towel, sun cream, a hat, swimming goggles, a shell, some stones. Put these on a central table.
Write on the board:
Boy: Can you help me?
Girl: Of course I can!
Learners work in groups. Point to the conversation and say *This is the start of a conversation. Write two or three more lines. Why did the boy need help? How did the girl help him? You choose.* Point to the beach objects and say *These might give you ideas!*
Learners copy the two lines of speech in their notebooks and continue the conversation. Groups act out their conversation in class, taking turns to use the props if they want to.

D Complete the questions with words from the box.

- Approach one learner and say *Your name's (Maria), isn't it?* In L1, ask learners how this kind of question is different from *Is your name (Maria)?* (asking for confirmation of known information / asking for confirmation) Write on the board *It is, isn't it?* and *We haven't, have we?* so learners clearly see the pattern of repeated subject and the negative form coming first or last.

- Point to your chair and ask *And what is this? It is a chair, isn't it?* (yes) Show two of your pencils and say *They are mine, aren't they?* (yes)

- Point to a few items that belong to learners, e.g. a sweater or some books, and say *This is a sweater ...* (isn't it?) Say *These are (Maria)'s books ...* (aren't they?)

- Learners find tag questions in the story and circle them.

- Look at Activity D. Do the example with the class. Ask in L1 *Why is the first answer 'isn't it'?* (because the sentence begins with *It's*)

- In pairs or on their own, learners complete questions 2–6.

- Check answers in open class. Ask *Why is the second answer 'aren't they'?* (because for *These shells are* we can say *They are*)

Answers

2 aren't they   **3** isn't it   **4** haven't they   **5** isn't he
6 hasn't she

E Look at the picture on page 21. Listen and colour.

- Learners look at the picture on page 21. Say *Tell me about this picture.* Learners talk about the picture, e.g. *There are three birds. There are shells and stones. There's a pool between the rocks. Emma is looking in the pool. The boy is looking at Emma. We can see the sea.*

- Check that learners have crayons or colouring pencils.

- Say *Now let's listen to a boy and his teacher. They are talking about colouring four things in this picture. Sometimes the boy chooses the part of the picture or the colour. But sometimes his teacher says he must colour something different or use a different colour. Listen carefully.*

Test tip: FLYERS
Reading and Writing (Part 3)

✔ Three of the four colouring instructions might include a change of object or colour.

07

- Play the audio twice if necessary. Give learners time to finish colouring and to compare their pictures with a partner.

- Check answers in open class, asking, e.g. *What's red?* (the boy's scarf) *What's orange?* (the largest shell)

- Ask more questions about the picture and encourage learners to answer imaginatively: *What are the children saying? What is in the boy's bag? Why is Emma smiling?*

Answers

the boy's scarf – red
the largest shell – orange
the boy's fingers – pink
the rock above the boy's head – yellow

Tapescript:

Woman:		Let's add some colour to this picture now.
Boy:		Yes! I can do that. I'd like to colour the largest bird in the sky first.
Woman:		Good idea. Make it blue.
Boy:		Could I colour it green instead?
Woman:		All right!

Can you see the green bird? This is an example. Now you listen and colour.

1	**Boy:**	Can I colour the boy's bag next?
	Woman:	No. Colour his scarf instead, please.
	Boy:	Sure! What colour shall I use for that?
	Woman:	Red might look good. What do you think?
	Boy:	Yes! There!

2	**Woman:**	How about colouring a shell next?
	Boy:	OK. One of the shells in the water is huge. Can I colour that one?
	Woman:	Sure. Use your brown colour for that.
	Boy:	Sorry! Can I colour it orange instead?
	Woman:	Ha ha ha! All right!
3	**Boy:**	What now?
	Woman:	You can see the boy's fingers, but only on his left hand. Colour those, please.
	Boy:	OK. Let's make them purple.
	Woman:	Erm ... no, that might look strange. Colour them pink instead.
	Boy:	Fine! No problem.
4	**Boy:**	Let's colour a rock next. The one that's behind Emma?
	Woman:	Not that one. Colour the one above the boy's head.
	Boy:	Right! Shall I make it yellow?
	Woman:	If you want! Yes!
	Boy:	Thanks!

F Look at the pictures. Complete the story.

- Say *Look at the pictures. How many things can you see that begin with 's'?* Write learners' suggestions on the board, e.g. *sun, sea, sand, shark, stones, shells, seat, sky, skirt, star fish, sails, sailing boat, sweater, shoulders, shorts.*

- Ask *Where are these people? Is this a funny or sad story?* (learners answer) *It's called 'Oliver's shark'.* Point to the first gap and ask *What does Oliver like doing with his shark?* (e.g. playing and swimming with it) Say *Now you! Write words to complete the story.* Tell learners they can write more than one word in each gap. Learners work in pairs.

- Choose three or four pairs to read out their completed stories.

Suggested story

Oliver has a toy shark. He likes ***playing and swimming*** with it.
Last ***Saturday***, Oliver took his shark to ***his favourite beach***.
Emma and her friend, ***Paul White***, were in their sailing boat. ***Paul*** was afraid when he saw the shark.
'***Help! A dangerous shark!***' he shouted.
Oliver swam to the boat and held up his toy shark.
'***Don't worry! It's a toy!***' Oliver said. Everyone laughed a lot after that.

Extension

Write questions on the board about picture 1 for learners to think about:
Where is this beach? What time is it? How did this boy and his mother get to the beach? What is the boy saying to his mother? What is the mother saying? What is in the mother's beach bag? What is she reading about?
Pairs choose answers to the questions and write them in their notebooks. Ask different pairs to tell the class two or three of their answers.

G Listen and tick (✔) the box.

08

- With books closed, review/teach key vocabulary for the task. Mime *to swing, to skip, fishing* and *volleyball*. Use your skipping rope and toy fishing rod if you have them. Write *I'm cycling on my bicycle!* on the board. Mime *cycling*. Explain that there is no difference in meaning between *bike* and *bicycle*, but most people say *bike*.

- Say *Emma's talking to her mother and her father about things they can do on holiday.*

- With books open, learners look at the pictures in Activity G. Say *These are things Emma might do.* Ask *Which sports here need a ball?* (table tennis, hockey, volleyball, baseball) *Which must you do in or on water?* (swimming, fishing, sailing) *Which might you do in a park?* (swinging, roller skating, skipping, going for a walk, cycling)

- Say *Now listen and tick the correct picture: A, B or C.*

- Play the audio. Learners listen and tick.

- Learners compare their answers in pairs, before checking in open class. Ask *Number 1. What do Emma and Dad both want to do now?* Encourage learners to answer in full sentences (*They want to play … She wants to …*).

Answers

1 A   2 B   3 A   4 B

Tapescript:

1   What do Emma and Dad both want to do now?
    Dad: This is a lovely place, isn't it, Emma?
    Emma: Yes, Dad!
    Dad: You could go and play on those swings.
    Emma: I'm too old for that! We could go back to the beach for a swim instead.
    Dad: We can't do that now. The water isn't warm enough. Let's play table tennis.
    Emma: Great! I can use my amazing new bat.

2   What does Emma want to do this morning?
    Mum: Look, Emma. They're playing hockey over there. We could go and watch.
    Emma: You go, Mum, but I don't want to. I'd like to roller skate around the hotel garden instead this morning.
    Mum: Or you could do some skipping.
    Emma: No, it's too hot to do that.

3   What do Dad and Emma want to do next?
    Dad: I really enjoyed our ride around the lake yesterday, Emma.
    Emma: Me too. What do you want to do next?
    Dad: We could play volleyball but that's not your favourite sport, is it?
    Emma: No. Let's go for a walk in the woods with our rucksacks instead, Dad.
    Dad: That's a great idea!

4   What does Emma want to do after lunch?
    Mum: We could go fishing after lunch, Emma. We might catch a big fish!
    Emma: Let's go sailing instead, Mum. I'd like to do that.
    Mum: OK. Or we could play baseball with Dad?
    Emma: No. He wants to sit in the sun this afternoon.
    Mum: All right!

Extension

Say *You are on holiday. What activities do you want to do?* Write *Let's … We could …* on the board. In pairs, learners create a short conversation (four or five turns only). Encourage them to use other language from the activity, e.g. *All right! Great! OK! Of course! I'd enjoy … more. Or we could …* Ask two or three pairs to role play their conversations.

H Find words in the story that sound like these words.

- Say *Some words sound the same.* Learners look at Activity H. Read out the example so learners clearly hear that *glove* sounds like *love*. Explain in L1 that all the answers sound like the words in bold font.

- Explain in L1 that all the answers are important words in the story and sound like the words in bold font. Learners write answers to questions 2–6.
- Check answers. Ask *Which answers have spellings that look very different at the end?* (show/toe, talk/fork)

Answers

2 a ship **3** a toe **4** a fork **5** a stone **6** a wave

Extension

On the board, write the following words inside four big circles: *sea, shoe, door, hair*. Pairs choose two words and copy their circles in their notebooks. They then add other words that sound the same.

Suggested answers (words on YLE word list)

sea – pea, me, she, we, he, be, bee, see, knee, tree, three, ski, kiwi, taxi, key
shoe – do, who, to, too, zoo, through, glue, you, Sue, drew, grew
door – poor, floor, or, for, more, sore, store, score, wore, your, saw, draw, sure
hair – air, fair, chair, stair, square, bear, wear, where, there, their

Guess the words. Then listen and write.

26

- Learners look at the picture. Say *The pirate's son looks really …* (happy) *Why do most people feel happy when they are at the beach? What can they do there?* (learners answer)
- Learners look at the poem. Review/Teach *salty* and *explore*. Ask *What are the missing words? Guess.* Learners guess in pairs. They could write them in the gaps in pencil. Say *Let's listen to the pirate's happy poem now.*

09

- Play the audio once and then ask *Were your words the same?* Play the audio again. Learners correct any wrong answers.
- Check answers in open class. Learners then say the poem in chorus. Ask *Do you like eating fish and chips?* Stronger learners could write a fourth verse in their notebooks about what they enjoy doing at the seaside.

Answers

1 looking **2** talk **3** finding **4** hide **5** catching **6** eat

Tapescript:

See SB page 27 and Answers above.

Let's have fun!

Make a treasure map.

Learners look at page 69, Activity 3. Ask *What's this?* (a treasure map)

Say *Now it's your turn to make a treasure map. What things can you put on your map?* Learners read the ideas and choose what they want to include.

Give each learner a piece of paper. Learners draw and colour their maps. Ask *Where is the treasure? Draw a cross.* When their maps are complete, learners could make them look older by colouring or painting the edges of the paper yellow or brown.

Display the treasure maps in class. Encourage learners to look at the other maps and talk about the treasure. Ask *What is the treasure? Where did the pirates hide it?*

Let's speak!

Ask and answer questions about a really happy day.

Ask *When are you happy? Think of a really happy day.* Ask a few learners to tell you about it: *Where did you go? Who were you with? What did you enjoy doing?*

Provide the following prompts on the board:
Where did you go?
How did you get there?
What did you enjoy doing?
Why were you so happy?

Learners look at page 72, Activity 3. In pairs, they use the questions to talk about their happy day.

Learners tell the class about their own or their partner's happy day (e.g. *Luis went to the park with his family. They went there on the bus. They had a picnic. He was happy because his friends were there too.*)

Let's say! Page 74

Say *Look at page 74, Activity 3. Listen.* Play the audio. Say *Let's say* /s/. *Pirate's, son, nice, mouse, sailing, across, sea, glass, box.* Learners repeat.
Say *Tell me more English words with* /s/. Learners answer (e.g. sail, sausage, silly, seven). Learners listen again to the audio, repeating the rhyme as fast as they can.

Home FUN booklet

➡ **Pages 8–9, the body and the face**
➡ **Picture dictionary: the body and the face, clothes**

Go online

to practise your English
to listen to the audio recordings
to find more FUN activities!

The king's colours

4

Main topics:	animals, colours, natural world, materials
Story summary:	The king is sad because there are so few colours in his country. A strange old lady finds a way to help make the king happy again.
Main grammar:	*make somebody/something* + adjective, *be made of, Where* clauses
Main vocabulary:	*beetle, begin, butterfly, camel, eagle, enough, everywhere, excellent, hill, interesting, journey, king, lovely, midday, stone, strawberry, thousand, touch, wings, wish, wonderful*
Value:	Being patient ("*I can wait. I don't mind.*")
Let's say!:	/r/
Practice for Flyers:	Reading and Writing Part 1 (A), Reading and Writing Part 5 (B), Listening Part 2 (E), Speaking Parts 2 and 4 (F), Listening Part 3 (G)
Equipment:	• ▶ audio: Storytelling, E, G, I, Let's say! • → (presentation **PLUS**) flashcards Go to Presentation plus to find pictures of Flyers vocabulary from Unit 4. You can use the pictures to teach/review important words in this unit.	• → (presentation **PLUS**) Image carousel 19–28 (beetle, butterfly, camel, eagle, hippo, horse, snake, swan, tiger, wolf): Storytelling, A Extension • Photocopy 4, one per learner (TB page 57): Let's have fun! • crayons or colouring pencils: Let's have fun!

 Storytelling

Before listening

With books closed …

- Introduce the topic of the story. Ask *What's your favourite colour?* Write the colours learners suggest on the board. Ask about different colours, e.g. *Which animal/food is that colour?* Say *This story is about a king who is unhappy because there aren't many colours in his country.*
- Ask *How many yellow/grey animals can you think of?* (learners suggest ideas)
- Review/Teach *camel, swan, eagle, horse, hippo, snake, wolf, butterfly, beetle* and *tiger*, using the Image carousel.
- Review/Teach the word *patient*. Demonstrate by miming waiting for a bus patiently (*I am being patient*) and waiting impatiently, looking at your watch, pacing up and down (*I am not being patient*).
- Remember you can use the flashcards on Presentation plus to help you teach and review vocabulary.
- Look at the first story picture without the story text on the Image carousel or with the story text in the book on page 28. Ask *Which animals can you see?* (horses, eagles, a snake) *What's the weather like?* Say *The man is the king. What colours can you see in this countryside? Does his country look like ours? Why? / Why not?* Learners answer.
- Say *Now let's listen to the story.* Say *Let's look at page 28.*

Listening

With books open …

▶
10

- Play the audio or read the story. Learners listen.
- Play the audio or read the story again.
- Pause after *These three colours could make me the happiest king in the world* on page 29. Ask *Why was the king sad?* (there weren't many colours in his country) *Who hears the king?* (an old woman) *How long does she walk to speak to him?* (three days) *What can she give the king?* (more colours) *What colours does he ask for?* (orange, black and white) *What do you know that is orange or black or white? What do you know that is all three colours?* (learners suggest ideas)
- Pause after *The orange butterfly, the black beetle and the white wolf followed him on his long journey* on page 30. Ask *Which animals come to see the king?* (an orange butterfly, a black beetle and a white wolf) *What does the king want now?* (a black, white and orange animal) *What must he climb?* (the highest hill) *What food must he find?* (an orange fruit, five black beans and some white bread)
- At the end of the story, ask *How long did the king wait next to the old woman's rock?* (three weeks) *What touches his back?* (a tiger) *How does the king feel then?* (happy) *What other colours begin to appear?* (red, purple, green)

After listening

- After listening to the whole story, ask *Is the king patient?* (yes) *Why is he happy at the end of the story? Because there are more …* (colours in his country now) *What do you think are the best new animals or plants in the story?* (learners suggest ideas)

A Read and write the word.

- Review/Teach the animal words. *Tortoise* and *insect* may be new words. Ask *Which animals live in sandy deserts?* (camels) *Which are birds?* (eagle, swan) *Which are all kinds of insects?* (beetles, butterflies, insects) *Which can swim?* (swans) *Which move really slowly?* (tortoises) Ask different learners to choose an animal and mime it for the class to guess.

- Learners look at Activity A. Ask *How many answers are there above the sentences?* (seven) *How many sentences are there?* (six) Say *So you don't need one of these answers.*

- Learners work on their own to match the words and definitions, and then compare their answers.

- Check answers. Ask, e.g. *Which animal has a long neck?* (a swan) *Which animal might have spots on its wings?* (a butterfly) *Which bird might build a nest on a mountain?* (an eagle)

- Ask *Which is the wrong answer?* (an insect)

Answers

2 a tortoise   **3** a swan   **4** a butterfly   **5** an eagle
6 a beetle

Test tip: FLYERS
Reading and Writing (Part 1)

✔ Learners have to read and understand ten clues and match them to ten nouns. Learners should read the definitions carefully. There will be 15 answers to choose from. The nouns may come from three or four different topic sets. Many nouns will be singular, but some may be uncountable or plural.

➜ When you are teaching a lexical set, e.g. animals, it is often useful to make links with other animals that are similar in some way. So if you are teaching *beetle*, you might also teach *butterfly* and the word *insects*. If you are teaching *swan*, teach *eagle* and revise Movers words *bat*, *parrot* and *penguin* at the same time, as these all have wings.

Extension

Write the following animals on the board: *tiger, hippo, snake, wolf* and then add these gapped sentences:
The colour of this animal is .... and it lives in ....
This animal has .... and it can ....
Learners complete the two sentences in their notebooks. Their partner then guesses the animal.

B Complete the sentences. Write 1, 2, 3 or 4 words.

- Say *Look at the pictures in the story.* Ask different learners *Which picture do you like most? What is happening in that part of the story?* (learners answer)

- Learners look at the picture in Activity B. Ask *What can you see?* (an orange, some black beans and some bread) *Why are these important in the story?* (the king must find these)

- Read aloud the instruction. Ask *Can you use one word to complete the sentences?* (yes) *Two?* (yes) *Five?* (no) *Four?* (yes) Review/Teach *ago* and then look at the example. Ask *When did the king live?* (thousands of years ago)

- Learners work in pairs to find the answers in the story and complete the sentences. Walk around and help if necessary. Make sure learners are not writing more than four words.

- Check answers in open class.

Answers

2 old woman   **3** orange, black and white   **4** the (highest) hill   **5** woke up   **6** purple sweet potato plants

Test tip: FLYERS
Reading and Writing (Part 5)

✔ Structures in the story text and in the sentences to be completed might be different. However, the words (1, 2, 3 or 4) that learners need to write should be copied from the story text. Learners will not need to change these to complete their answers.

➜ Give learners practice in transforming sentences, e.g. *Last **Wednesday**, Robert went skiing with his cousins. / Robert went skiing with his cousins on **Wednesday**. Sophia **made** her model dinosaur with card and paper. / Sophia's model dinosaur was **made** with card and paper. David hasn't **played football** for three weeks. / David last **played football** three weeks ago.*

Extension

Learners look at sentence 3 again. Learners work in small groups to discuss answers. Ask *Which new colours would you choose? Why? With your three new colours, what other things might appear in the king's country?*

C The king is a very patient person. What does he say?

- Mime frowning and pacing. Ask *Am I a patient person?* (no)

- Say *Look at the picture. Which animals are with the king?* (the wolf, the butterfly and the beetle) *Who is the king waiting for?* (the old woman)

- Ask *Which answer sounds the most patient? The king is a very patient person. What does he say?* (learners decide)

Suggested answer

B I don't mind. I can wait!

- Talk about the message of the story. See 'Value' above.

D Write about you. Find and choose the words.

- With books closed, mime different expressions, e.g. *happy, sad, tired, angry, worried, frightened.* Prompt answers by asking *How am I feeling? Am I afraid?*

- Write *happy, sad, tired, angry* on the board. Add other feeling adjectives that learners suggest.

- In L1 if necessary, explain the meaning of *opposite.* Then ask *What's the opposite of 'happy'? Is it sad or tired?* (sad) Review/Teach *unhappy.* Ask *What's the opposite of 'patient'?* (impatient)

- With books open, learners read the instruction. Say *Can you find seven words in the word snake?* Learners circle the words.

- Say *Now complete the sentences about you.* Learners share ideas in groups before they choose their own word to complete the sentences. They can choose other words if they want. Walk around and help with vocabulary if necessary.

- Ask for feedback in open class. Ask different learners to complete each sentence. Accept all valid answers.

Extension

With stronger learners, you could write the following sentence starters on the board for learners to copy and complete as homework, or in groups. They might also like to illustrate an answer with a drawing.
I feel afraid when …
I feel impatient when …
I feel pleased when …
I feel lucky when …

E Listen and write about Oliver.

- Point to the picture of the boy. Say *Look! This is Oliver. What did Oliver do with his father?* (a lot of travelling) *What was he listening to when he heard this story?* (the radio)

- Learners look at the form and the example. Ask *How old is Oliver?* (12) Point to the other prompts and ask *What do we need to know about Oliver?* (the name of his city, his favourite animal, what makes him happy, his web address) Ask *Where does he live? What is his favourite animal? Guess!* (learners guess) Say *Now listen to a boy and a girl. They're talking about Oliver.*

- Play the audio. Learners listen and write the answers.
- Learners compare their answers in pairs. Play the audio again if needed.

11

Answers

2 Hatleigh   **3** octopus   **4** swimming
5 www.olanimalstories.com

Tapescript:

Boy:	I know Oliver and I really liked listening to this story too.
Girl:	Did you? Tell me more about Oliver. How old is he?
Boy:	He's twelve now, so he's one year older than us.
Can you see the answer? Now listen and write.	
Girl:	Where does he live?

Boy:	He lives in a city called Hatleigh.
Girl:	How do you spell that? Can you tell me?
Boy:	Of course! It's H-A-T-L-E-I-G-H.
Girl:	Uh! I don't know that place.
Boy:	Well, you can find it on one of the online maps.
Girl:	OK. Does Oliver like animals? Has he got a favourite?
Boy:	Yes! He loves reading about octopuses.
Girl:	Really?
Boy:	Yes. He likes drawing them too. Did you know that octopuses have three hearts!
Girl:	No! Why?
Boy:	I'm not sure. Perhaps we should find out.
Girl:	Yes! What makes Oliver happiest?
Boy:	He loves swimming.
Girl:	So do I!
Boy:	Me too!
Girl:	And did Oliver write about any other stories?
Boy:	Yes. On his website. I've got his web address here. It's www dot then OL animal stories dot com. Shall I repeat that?
Girl:	Yes, please.
Boy:	OK. www dot OL animal stories dot com.
Girl:	Great! Thanks.

F Ask and answer questions about pets.

- Ask learners *Have you got a pet? What is its name? How old is it? What's your favourite kind of pet?*

- In open class, look at the question prompts for Oliver's pet. Write on the board *What kind .... animal ....?* In L1, explain to learners they can make the question by adding words. Point to the gaps and ask *What's this question?* (What kind of animal is Oliver's pet?)

- Learners expand the other notes in the same way. Write the five questions on the board.

- Divide learners into A and B pairs. Learner A holds the book as normal. Learner B holds the book upside down to read the task. Ask one pair to demonstrate this. Learner A asks questions about Oliver's pet. Learner B answers. Learner B then asks about Sophia's pet and Learner A answers.

- Feed back in open class. Ask A learners to talk about Oliver's pet. Ask B learners to talk about Sophia's pet.

Answers

Sophia's pet is a mouse. It is called Fred. It is white and pink. It is small. It is six months old.
Oliver's pet is a bird. It is called Betty. It is red and yellow. It is large. It is three years old.

✔ The examiner asks the learner for some information about a visit, party, etc. but not necessarily in the same order as the learner's information is listed. Give learners practice in matching questions and answers.

➔ Write five pieces of information on the board, e.g. any date, time, name of a place, activity and mode of transport. In pairs, learners think of questions to ask about each piece of information and write the conversation. Tell learners to list their questions in any order. Pairs then role play their conversations in open class.

Extension

In small groups, learners ask and answer questions about each other's pets (real or imagined), using the same questions and others if they wish, e.g. *What does it like eating? Where does it sleep?*

Sophie is talking to Mr Fisher about pictures of animals on her clothes. Where is each animal? Listen and write a letter in each box.

• Learners look at the animal pictures. Ask *What do you know about these animals?* Learners answer.

• Say *Listen to Sophie. She is talking to her teacher, Mr Fisher, about her favourite animals and her clothes. Where is each animal? Listen and write the letter in each animal box. Let's look at the example first. Which letter is next to the camel?* (D)

12

• Play the audio twice.

• Learners compare their answers in pairs.

• Check answers in open class, asking, e.g. *Where is the picture of the beetle?* (on Sophie's gloves) *Where is the swan?* (on Sophie's necklace)

• Listen again, pausing after each mini-conversation.

• After the one about camels, ask *Where are our 'eyelashes'?* Learners guess. Point to your eyelashes or draw an eye with eyelashes on the board.

• After the one about swans, ask *What are 'feathers'?* Learners guess. Draw a feather on the board.

• After the one about tortoises, ask *What does 'smell' mean?* Learners guess. Mime *smell*.

• After the one about beetles, ask *What does 'wood' mean?* Learners guess. Point to wooden objects in the classroom, e.g. tables or the floor.

• After the last mini-conversation, ask *What does 'taste' mean?* Learners guess. Mime tasting an ice cream and say *Mmm, delicious! It tastes good!*

• Then ask *Did you learn anything new? What did you learn about butterflies?* (they can taste with their feet) *What about beetles?* (they eat wood), etc.

Answers

beetle F   swan C   butterfly E   tortoise A

Man:	You're very interested in animals, aren't you, Sophie?
Girl:	Yes, Mr Fisher. I really like camels. I've got one of those on my favourite sweater!
Man:	Really?
Girl:	Yes! Camels have lots and lots of eyelashes to stop sand going into their eyes!

Can you see the letter D? Now you listen and write a letter in each box.

Girl:	I like swans too. Do you know, a swan has more than 25,000 feathers on its body!
Man:	That's amazing!
Girl:	I've got a necklace with a little gold swan on it.
Man:	That's nice!
Man:	What other animals do you like learning about?
Girl:	Tortoises! They don't smell with their noses.
Man:	Don't they?
Girl:	No! They smell with the back of their mouths! They have to open their mouths first, of course.
Man:	What an interesting creature!
Girl:	It is, isn't it? I've got one on my new trainers. … Sorry, I mean on my new umbrella!
Man:	Do you like beetles too?
Girl:	Oh, yes! I like big black ones most of all. I've got some funny beetles on my gloves that Grandma made for me. They're made of wool.
Man:	Brilliant.
Girl:	And beetles eat other insects, but they also eat wood!
Man:	Oh!
Man:	And I know you like butterflies.
Girl:	Well, they're really pretty, aren't they?
Man:	So tell me something interesting about those.
Girl:	Well, I've got one on my belt and they can taste with their feet! Oh! And a butterfly uses glue to glue its eggs to a leaf!
Man:	Well, thanks for teaching me something new!
Girl:	Ha ha ha!

✔ In the second set of pictures, two pictures will not be needed, but will be heard in the conversation. Train learners to be aware of and spot incorrect answers.

➔ When you are playing the audio, pause after a conversation turn where you hear something about a right and a wrong answer. Ask *Which is the right answer?* Learners answer. *Why is (the umbrella) the right answer? Why is (trainers) the wrong answer?*

Complete the crossword.

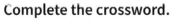
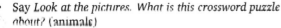

- Say *Look at the pictures. What is this crossword puzzle about?* (animals)
- Ask *Which small animals have four pretty wings?* (butterflies) Say *This word can help you with the other spellings.*
- Learners work in pairs to complete the crossword. You could make this a race.
- Walk around and check spelling. Check answers in open class.

> **Answers**
>
> **1** creatures **2** camel **3** eagle **4** insects
> **5** octopus **6** tortoise **7** dinosaur **8** beetles **9** swans

> **Extension**
>
> Play an animal word chain game. Learners take turns to say an animal. They must say an animal beginning with the same letter as the last letter of the previous animal. They can ask to add an *–s* for plurals to the last animal if necessary, e.g.
> *snake – elephant – tiger – rabbits – shark …*
> To make this easier, write the words on the board as learners say them. Learners should not repeat words, but they can ask classmates to help them. The game continues until learners run out of animals they know. Learners can write and illustrate their own animal chain in their notebooks for homework. Ask *Who can write more than six animals?*

> **Possible answer (16 words):**
>
> bird donkeys snake eagle elephants shark kangaroo octopus sheep penguins snail lizard dinosaur rabbit tigers spider

Listen and write the words.

- Say *Let's read the travel poem.* Read the text aloud, pausing for learners to suggest answers for the gaps.
- Play the audio. Learners listen and write the missing words. Play the audio a second time for learners to check their answers.

13

- Ask learners to suggest actions for the poem. Practise these together, e.g.

Can you feel the north wind on your face?	blow air
Hold on to your hat!	hands on heads
Now we're walking through the grass	mime wading through long grass

- Learners chant the poem as a class with actions and mimes. If possible, learners walk around the classroom while they chant the poem.

> **Answers**
>
> **2** grass **3** socks **4** back **5** brave **6** tiger **7** problem

> **Tapescript:**
>
> See SB page 35 and Answers above.

Let's have fun!

Write an animal fact file.

With books closed, ask *What do you know about hippos?* Learners suggest ideas. (they are very big, they can swim, they are grey or brown)

Learners look at page 69, Activity 4. Say *Read the fact file about hippos.* After learners have finished reading, ask *What new information did you learn? What did you already know?*

Now read the instruction and the bullet points aloud. Ask *What do you have to do?* (choose an animal, find out about it and draw a picture of it)

Give each learner a copy of Photocopy 4 (TB page 57). They research their chosen animal and make a poster showing their information and picture. Display the posters in the classroom if possible.

Let's speak!

Ask and answer the questions about your favourite animal.

Provide the following prompts on the board:
What's your favourite wild animal?
Where does it live?
What does it eat?
Why do you like it?
Say something else about your favourite animal.

Learners look at page 72, Activity 4. They read the instruction and the questions. In open class, ask learners for suggestions about what kind of information they could add for the *Say something else* prompt. (e.g. size, number of legs, colour, noise it makes)

Ask different learners *What's your favourite wild animal? Why do you like those?*

In pairs, learners take turns to ask and answer the questions on the board. They report back in open class. Ask *Did you see this animal in a zoo? In the countryside?*

27

> **Let's say! Page 74**
>
> Say *Look at page 74, Activity 4. Listen.* Play the audio. Say *Let's say /r/. Front, mirror, grey, rock, rain, wrote, brilliant, story, three, red, strawberries.* Learners repeat.
> Say *Tell me more English words with /r/.* Learners answer (e.g. robot, ring, radio). Learners listen again to the audio, repeating the rhyme as fast as they can.

> 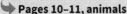 **Home FUN booklet**
>
> 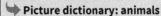 **Pages 10–11, animals**
> ➡ **Picture dictionary: animals**

> **Go online**
>
> to practise your English
> to listen to the audio recordings
> to find more FUN activities!

Robert's envelopes

5

Main topics:	places and transport
Story summary:	Robert lives in the city. He wants to have a holiday in the countryside, but he and his mother don't have enough money. One day, a special message changes everything.
Main grammar:	conjunctions: *if, so, after* + clause
Main vocabulary:	*across, bank, bridge, building, chemist, envelope, factory, finish, flag, front, hotel, low, middle, motorway, noisy, over, pocket, police station, post office, pyjamas, skyscraper, somewhere, strange, stream, taxi, unhappy, woods*
Value:	Hoping to achieve an ambition (*"One day, perhaps!"*)
Let's say!:	/dʒ/
Practice for Flyers:	Reading and Writing Part 1 (A), Speaking Part 1 (F), Reading and Writing Part 6 (G), Listening Part 1 (H), Reading and Writing Part 4 (J)

Equipment:	• ▶ audio: Storytelling, H, Let's say! • flashcards Go to Presentation plus to find pictures of Flyers vocabulary from Unit 5. You can use the pictures to teach/review important words in this unit.	• ➡ presentation **PLUS** Image carousel 29–32 (beak, building, message, ship): Storytelling • Photocopy 5, one per learner (TB page 58): D Extension • crayons or colouring pencils: D Extension, F (optional) • phone or tablet to record learners' vlogs: Let's have fun! • paper (one sheet per learner): E Extension, Let's speak! • three different books: J

✦ Storytelling

Before listening

With books closed …

- Introduce the topic of the story by asking learners *Do you enjoy going on holiday? Where do you like going? How do you like to travel?* (by bus, train, plane) Write their suggestions on the board.
- Ask *Why do you enjoy travelling like this?* (it's fast/nice/exciting/fun)
- Use the photographs on the Image carousel to review/teach *building, ship, beak* and *message*. Review/Teach *skyscraper, traffic, motorway* and *ocean*. Ask questions to check understanding, e.g. *Is a skyscraper a high or low building?* (high) *You're trying to cross a busy city street, but there's too much …* (traffic) *Traffic might travel slowly along a road, but very fast along a …* (motorway) *Is an ocean usually bigger or smaller than a sea?* (bigger) Remember you can use the flashcards on Presentation plus to help you teach and review vocabulary.
- Look at the first story picture without the story text on the Image carousel or with the story text in the book on page 36. Ask *What is this story about?* (a boy) *Where does this boy live?* (in a city) *Who is he with?* (his mother) *Where are they now?* (in their living room)
- Say *This story is about a boy called Robert who wants to travel to exciting places.* Say *Now let's listen to the story.* Say *Let's look at page 36.*

Listening

With books open …

14
- Play the audio or read the story. Learners listen.
- Play the audio or read the story again.
- Pause after *'I could look out of its windows at the woods and mountains below,' he thought* on page 37. Ask *Where is Robert going?* (to school) *Where is Robert now?* (on a bus) *What can he see through the window?* (the city / buildings / a bridge / the river / a boat / a train / a plane)
- Pause again after *'If you find this message, go and look in your biggest, oldest book'* on page 38. Ask *What is Robert reading?* (the bird's message) *Where must Robert look for something?* (in his biggest, oldest book) *How old is the book perhaps?* (learners guess) *What might Robert find in the book?* (learners guess)

After listening

- Talk about the story. Ask *Why can Robert and his mother go on holiday now?* (they have got enough money) *Why is Robert looking at the sky and thinking 'Thank you'?* (he is thanking the bird) *Where can Robert and his mother go on holiday now?* (learners guess)

- In L1, say *Robert had an ambition. He hoped that one day he could travel to exciting places. Did he give up hope?* (no) *Is he angry with his mother because they had to stay in the city in his summer holidays before?* (no) Say *Robert understood that it was difficult for his mother to take him on holiday, but was he optimistic?* (yes) *What did he say?* ('One day, perhaps!') Ask *Is it important to have a dream for the future? Why?* Accept answers in English or L1.

 A

Read and complete the words.

- Learners look at the example. Ask *Why do people use a lift to get to the top of this building?* (it is very tall) Say *Find 'skyscrapers' in the story.* Learners find and underline the word on page 36. Say *Now you! Read the sentences and write the words from the story.* Learners work in pairs. They can check spelling of the words in the story. Check answers in open class.

Answers

2 traffic   **3** a motorway   **4** a hospital   **5** a hotel
6 a bridge

Extension

In pairs, learners choose another noun from the story, and write a simple definition for another pair to guess. For support, you could write on the board:
This is a kind of …
This is a word for …
You can … with this.
Walk around and help with vocabulary or grammar if necessary.

 B

Read and answer the questions. Write 2 or 3 words.

- With books closed, ask *Which important things can you remember in the story?* Learners suggest main events, e.g. *Robert gets a message. He finds a little card. His mum takes the card to the bank. They have more money at the end of the story. They can go on holiday.*

- Learners look at Activity B. Ask *How many words can you write in each answer?* (two or three) Learners look at the example question and its answer.

- In pairs, learners try to remember the answers for questions 2–5 and write them on the dotted lines. They can check their answers in the story.

- Ask *Did you remember all the answers? Which ones did you forget?* Learners answer. Check the answers with the class by asking *Did Robert stay in a hotel last summer?* (no) *What was black and white?* (the bird) *Who was Helen Bird?* (Robert's mother's grandmother) *Where does Mr Flag work?* (in the bank)

Answers

2 at home / in the city   **3** black and white   **4** Helen Bird   **5** Mr Flag

 C

Put the pictures in order. Write numbers.

- With books closed, show learners the story pictures from the Image carousel, in a different order. Ask *What happened in the story? Which picture is first?* (Robert and his mother in their living room) *Which picture is next?* (Robert on the bus) *And then?* (Robert reading the message) *And then?* (Robert standing on a chair, getting the book) *And which is the last picture?* (Robert holding the tickets)

- Learners look at the pictures in Activity C. Ask *What can you see here?* Learners describe the pictures, e.g.
  - A – The bird and the message.
  - B – Robert's finding something in the big book.
  - C – Robert's getting on a bus.
  - D – Robert's carrying a chair to the bookcase.
  - E – Robert's mum is talking to Mr Flag.
  - F – Robert's sitting on the wall.

- Say *Find the picture that starts the story. Can you see the number 1 in its box? Now you order the other pictures. Write the numbers.* Learners work on their own, and then check their answers in pairs.

- Ask *Which is the second picture? Which is the third? Where's the fourth?* etc. Then check answers.

Answers

A 3   B 5   C (1)   D 4   E 6   F 2

- Then point to picture C and ask *What did Robert see in the river when he was on the bus?* (a boat)
  Write on the board:
  After Robert got on the bus, he saw the boat on the river.
  Say *We can also say 'Robert saw the boat on the river after he got on the bus.'* Write that sentence too.

- Write the following sentence starters for learners to complete in their notebooks:
  After the bird arrived with the envelope, …
  After Robert read the message, …
  After Robert's mother spoke to Mr Flag, …

- In pairs, learners find things in the story pictures that begin with *b*. Each pair then works with another pair to increase their lists. Ask for answers. Learners spell the words. Write them on the board: *boy, balcony, books, bag, bookcase; bus, boat, bridge; ball; bowl.*

Extension

Divide learners into groups of four or five. In their groups, learners take turns to retell the story. They must include some information which is not true. The other group members listen and interrupt when they hear something wrong. Then the next learner continues telling the story from the same place, e.g.

Learner A:	*Robert lived in the countryside.*
Learner B:	*No! He lived in the city!* *Robert went on holiday every year.*
Learner C:	*No! He never went on holiday!* *Robert went to school on the train.*
Learner D:	*No! He went on the bus!*

 D

What does Robert want to do? Tick (✔) the correct boxes.

- Ask *What would Robert like to do one day?* (go on a boat, a fast train and a plane)

- Learners look at the sentences and tick the correct boxes.
- Then ask different learners to read out their ticked answers in full sentences beginning with *He wants to … / He'd like to …*
- Ask different learners *Would you like to do these things too?*

Answers

travel along a river, sail across the sea, cross a high bridge, fly somewhere in a plane

- Write *What <u>would you like</u> to do one day? <u>I'd like</u> to …* on the board. Explain that *I'd* is a short way of saying *I would.*
- In pairs, learners ask *What would you like to do one day?* and answer. Walk around and help with vocabulary if necessary. Learners write their answers in their notebooks. Check their answers in open class.

Extension: Photocopy 5

Divide learners into groups of three or four. Give each learner Photocopy 5 (TB page 58).
Learners look at the prompts and choose three things they would each like to do. They tell others in their group. In open class, ask two or three learners what their ideas are.
Learners complete the sentences and draw a picture of themselves to illustrate their answers.

E Complete the sentences with your own words.

- Review/Teach *if*. Explain that (at this level) zero conditional *if* can mean the same as *when*. Then write on the board:

  If you are feeling hungry …
- Ask *What can you do if you feel hungry?* Ask a learner to come to the board to finish writing the sentence.
- Learners look at Activity E and read the example.
- Say *Now you complete the sentences.* Walk around and help with vocabulary if necessary.
- Learners compare their answers in pairs.

Possible answers

If you are feeling tired, go to bed. If you want to catch a train, go to the railway station. If you need some more money, go to the bank.

Extension

Give each learner a piece of paper. Write on the board:
If you are … If you want … If you feel …
If you need … If you eat … If you find …
Point and say *Choose one of these to start the first sentence. Write it at the top of your piece of paper.*
Learners copy the sentence starter. Then tell learners to pass their paper to another classmate who completes the sentence and then copies another sentence starter from the board. The paper is passed on again until there are six completed sentences on it, or for as long as learners are enjoying the game. Learners read out the funniest sentences.

F Look at the pictures. Find six differences.

- Learners look at the two pictures in Activity F. Ask *Why is Robert on this bus?* (he is travelling to school) *Does he always go to school on a bus?* (learners guess)
- Say *Some things in the two pictures are the same and some are different. In this picture,* (point to the picture on the left) *Robert is wearing a blue shirt, but in this picture* (on the right) *he is …* (wearing a brown and yellow sweater)
- Write this model on the board on two lines:

  In this picture, Robert is wearing a blue shirt,

  but in this picture, he is wearing a brown and yellow sweater.
- Practise this in open class.
- In pairs or small groups, learners find the other five differences and think how to describe them. Then groups take turns to tell the class one difference.

Suggested answers

In this picture, Robert is standing up, but in this picture, he is sitting down.
In this picture, the person in front of Robert is a man who is reading a newspaper, but in this picture, the person in front of Robert is a woman who is reading a book.
In this picture, there are two boats on the river, but in this picture, there is one boat on the river.
In this picture, there is a train on the bridge, but in this picture, there are cars and lorries on the bridge.
In this picture, it is cloudy, but in this picture, it is sunny.

Test tip: FLYERS
Speaking (Part 1)

✔ Learners talk about differences between two similar pictures.
→ Use the sets of three optional pictures from Listening Part 4 tasks to give learners further practice at comparing pictures. They could work in pairs and say and then write their differences, e.g. *In this picture, the girl is skiing, but in this picture she is snowboarding, and in this picture she is on a sledge.* Learners could also draw two pictures with four or five differences. These should be differences in the number, colour, position, activities or absence/presence of things or people. Learners talk about the differences in pairs and then write about them for homework.

G Complete the story with your own words.

- Say *Let's read a new story!* Read the story aloud, pausing at each gap for learners to suggest which words to add. Prompt if necessary, e.g. *Katy sat down for a minute on a yellow seat outside the …* (Post office? School? Airport? Shop?)
- Say *Now you complete the story.* Learners choose and write words to complete the text.
- Ask different learners to read out one of their completed sentences. Accept any valid answers.
- Develop the story further. Ask *Whose rucksack was it? Who wrote the message? What happened next? Where did Katy go?* Encourage creative answers.
- Ask *What is the most exciting thing you found?*

H Listen and draw lines.

- Learners look at the picture in Activity H. Ask *What is happening in this picture? What is inside all these letters?* Learners suggest ideas, e.g. party invitations. Ask *Can you see the line between the woman in the post office and 'Holly'?* Say *The woman's name is Holly*.

- Say *A girl is talking to her grandfather about the people in this picture. Listen and draw lines.*

15

- Play the audio twice.

- Learners compare their lines in pairs after listening. Then check answers in open class.

Answers

George – bird carrying letter
Katy – girl on bike
Frank – man driving van
Betty – woman in blue coat
Robert – boy on wall

Tapescript:

Man:	Do you know these people here?
Girl:	Yes, Grandpa. I know the woman in the post office. You can see her through the window … but it's quite difficult.
Man:	Yes, it is. What's her name?
Girl:	She's called Holly.
Man:	Oh! Well, she looks busy …

Can you see the line? This is an example. Now you listen and draw lines.

Girl:	If you want, we can buy some bread from this shop.
Man:	OK! Oh, look! There's a large brown bird. It's carrying one of these letters!
Girl:	Yes. It's funny, isn't it? I know that bird. It's called George.
Man:	Really?
Girl:	Yes!
Girl:	That girl is a friend of my sister's. She's wearing her new helmet. Look!
Man:	Yes. Where's she cycling to?
Girl:	I don't know, but her name's Katy.
Man:	That's a pretty name.

Man:	And who's that?
Girl:	The man in the bread shop?
Man:	No, the other one. The one with a baseball cap on his head.
Girl:	Oh, that's Frank. He's driving to the hospital, I think. He works there.
Man:	I might know that person. Is her name Sophia?
Girl:	The woman in the blue coat? No, she's called Betty.
Man:	Oh! I'm usually good at remembering names.
Girl:	Are you? I'm not!
Girl:	And there's Robert! He's sitting on that low wall.
Man:	Why's he doing that?
Girl:	Perhaps he's tired.
Man:	And are there letters in all these envelopes? There are lots here!

Extension

In small groups, learners develop information about this picture. Write the following questions on the board to help prompt ideas:
Where is Katy going to on her bike?
What's the name of the man in the bread shop?
What kind of work does Frank do at the hospital?
What's the old woman's favourite hobby?
Which other shops are in this street?
Groups could share their ideas in open class and then learners could write their own answers in their notebooks for homework.

I Find the opposite words in the story.

- Learners look at the example. Ask *What are 'small' and 'big'? Are they adjectives or verbs?* (adjectives) Explain in L1 if necessary that adjectives describe nouns. Say *All these words are adjectives. 'Big' is the opposite of 'small'.* Learners find *big* in the story (page 39) and underline it. Ask *What does 'big' describe here?* (the bird)

- In pairs, learners choose answers to words 2–9 and then find and underline their answers in the story. They write their answers on the dotted lines.

- Check answers (accept alternatives if valid) and write them on the board.

Extension

Pairs think of four more opposite pairs. Pairs take turns
to write two opposite adjectives on the board, e.g. *cold
– hot*. Ask different learners to include these adjectives
in a sentence, e.g. *I don't like cold drinks, but I love hot
chocolate!*

Suggested answers

bad – good, fast – slow, easy – difficult, high – low,
dark – light, left – right, dry – wet, empty – full

J Look and read. Choose the words.

- Hold up three different books. One is obviously the
  biggest and the oldest. Make statements about them
  to revise comparative and superlative adjectives.
  Make half your statements right and half wrong.
  Learners stand up if they think what you say is right,
  or sit down if they think it is wrong.

  Say:

  This book is big.

  This book is bigger than this book.

  This is the biggest book.

- Hold up the biggest and oldest book. Ask *Is this the
  biggest and oldest book?* (yes) *Does it look like the one
  that Robert found?* (yes/no)

- Learners read Robert's holiday postcard, but don't
  write answers in the gaps yet. Ask *Where is Robert's
  hotel?* (next to the waterfall) *Is he having a good
  holiday?* (yes)

- Point to the three possible answers and say *Choose
  the correct word and write it on the line.* You may
  prefer to do this in open class. Check answers
  together.

Answers

2 staying   **3** highest   **4** After   **5** lots
6 because   **7** friendlier   **8** If   **9** to   **10** It

- Ask *When you go away on holiday, do you send
  postcards or text messages to your friends? What do you
  write about in your holiday messages?* Learners answer.

- In pairs, learners think of one more short sentence
  to add to the postcard, e.g. *I took 100 photos with my
  new phone yesterday!* Pairs read out their suggestions.
  Accept any reasonable answers.

5 Let's have fun!

Make a holiday vlog.

Learners look at page 70, Activity 5. Ask *What is the
boy doing?* (climbing a mountain) Say *Imagine you
are on holiday. Let's make a video for your friends.
What can you talk about?* Learners read the questions
and plan their ideas in pairs. They practise giving
their talk. Walk around and help if necessary. When
learners are ready, they can video their vlog using a
phone or tablet. Watch all the class videos together.

5 Let's speak!

Talk about sending messages.

Say *Write a message for one of your classmates.* Model
the task by writing *Hi! How are you?* on a piece of
paper. Show it to the class and then fold it in half
and give it to one learner who reads it. Say *Write an
answer and give it back to me!* Read out the answer.

Give each learner a small piece of paper. Learners
write, fold and deliver messages to whoever they
want in class, and then answer any messages they
have received. Learners continue sending and
answering messages until they tire of the task. Write
extra messages for any students who aren't receiving
many messages, or who are quick to reply.

Provide the following prompts on the board:

*If you want to send messages to your friends, how do
you usually do that?*
Do you write letters sometimes? Why? / Why not?
Does anyone in your family send emails?
*Do you like sending texts? Are your texts usually short
or long?*
*Do you know what LOL, B4N, GR8 and NP mean in a
text message?*
*Do you prefer to send messages on social media
websites? Why? / Why not?*

Learners look at page 73, Activity 5. Say *Talk about
sending messages.* In pairs, learners read and answer
the questions. After a discussion of the questions,
pairs take turns to report their answers back in open
class.

Answers:

LOL means 'laugh out loud'. B4N means 'bye for now'.
GR8 means 'great'. NP means 'no problem'.

28

Let's say! Page 75

Say *Look at page 75, Activity 5. Listen.* Play the audio. Say
*Let's say /dʒ/. Jack, message, George, journey, dangerous,
jungle, huge, orange, giraffe.* Learners repeat.
Say *Tell me more English words with /dʒ/.* Learners answer
(e.g. jump, juice, jellyfish, gym, geography). Learners
listen again to the audio, repeating the rhyme as fast as
they can.

Home FUN booklet

➡ **Pages 14–15, places and directions**
➡ **Picture dictionary: places and buildings, transport**

Go online

to practise your English
to listen to the audio recordings
to find more FUN activities!

6 Lara and the mountain lion

Main topics:	health, work, natural world, sports, animals
Story summary:	Lara is not strong enough to climb the mountain with her cousins. She stops to rest and meets a friendly mountain lion.
Main grammar:	*so* (conjuction and adverb)
Main vocabulary:	*a few, alone, backpack, bandage, chat, conversation, cookie, follow, honey, keep, knee, no problem, no-one, path, same, snowboard, soon, sore, speak, special, spotted, together, view, x-ray*
Value:	Helping each other (*"How can I help you now?"*)
Let's say!:	/w/
Practice for Flyers:	Listening Part 2 (E), Reading and Writing Part 2 (G), Listening Part 3 (H)

Equipment:	• ▶ audio: Storytelling, E, H, I, Let's say! •  flashcards Go to Presentation plus to find pictures of Flyers vocabulary from Unit 6. You can use the pictures to teach/review important words in this unit.	• ⮕ (presentation **PLUS**) Image carousel 33–48 (bear, crocodile, eagle, elephant, fur, giraffe, hippo, kangaroo, monkey, mountain lion, panda, snake, ice hockey, skating, skiing, sledging): Storytelling, H • crayons or colouring pencils: C, Let's have fun! • Photocopy 6, one per learner (TB page 59): Let's speak! • large sheet of paper (one per group): Let's have fun!

✦ Storytelling

Before listening

With books closed …

- Introduce the topic of the story. Ask *Which wild animals do you know?* Show learners some photographs of wild animals from the Image carousel: bear, crocodile, eagle, elephant, giraffe, hippo, kangaroo, monkey, panda, snake and mountain lion.

- Ask *Would you like to see some of these wild animals? Why? / Why not? Which is the largest? Funniest? Scariest?*

- Tell learners something about mountain lions. Say *Mountain lions live in North and South America. They are not as big as lions and tigers. Their fur is usually silver or grey. They can run 70 kilometres in one hour and can jump 12 metres! They live for about ten years.*

- Check understanding by asking questions, e.g. *How far can a mountain lion jump?* (12 metres) Say *This story is about a girl called Lara who meets a mountain lion.*

- Review/Teach *unkind, furry, sick* and *wonderful*. Ask *What's the opposite of 'kind'?* (unkind) Remind learners that you can add *un-* to *kind, friendly* and *tidy* to give opposite meanings. Use the picture on the Image carousel to review/teach *fur* and *furry*. Ask *Which animals are furry?* (e.g. bears, lions, tigers, rabbits) Mime looking ill and say *I'm ill. In America, people usually say I'm …* (sick) *What's another word for 'wonderful'?* (lovely, fantastic, brilliant, excellent) Remember you can use the flashcards on Presentation plus to help you teach and review vocabulary.

- Look at the first story picture without the story text on the Image carousel or with the story text in the book on page 44. Say *Tell me about the picture. What can you see?* (learners describe the picture) Ask *What do you think the story is about?* (learners guess)

- If necessary, prompt learners with more questions: *Who can you see?* (a woman and a boy) *What can you see on the wall?* (animal pictures, a newspaper story) *Who is Lara?* (learners guess) *What are Lara and the boy talking about?* (learners guess)

- Say *Now let's listen to the story.* Say *Let's look at page 44.*

Listening

With books open …

16

Play the audio or read the story. Learners listen.

Play the audio or read the story again.

Pause after '*The lion opened its mouth …*' at the end of page 44. Ask *What's Lara's job?* (vet / animal doctor) *Is Lara a grown-up or a child in this story?* (a child) *Who did Lara stay with in the winter holidays?* (her cousins) *Were her cousins kind to Lara?* (no) *What had a warm, furry face?* (the mountain lion)

- Pause again after *'How can I help you, now?'* at the end of page 45. Ask *What was wrong with the mountain lion?* (it was ill / it had a toothache/stomach-ache/headache) Review/Teach *medicine* and *handkerchief*. Ask *How did Lara help the lion?* (she gave it medicine / a cold handkerchief) *Is the lion better now?* (yes)

After listening

- After listening to the whole story, ask *Did the boy believe Lara's story? Why? / Why not?*
- Ask learners *Would you like to be a vet? What pets do vets look after?* (Learners suggest pets they know, e.g. kittens, puppies, rabbits, goldfish, parrots, tortoises and any other pets that your learners might have, such as hamsters or budgerigars.)

⭐ Value

- Say *Lara and the mountain lion helped each other. They were both kind.* Ask *How did Lara help the lion? What did she give it?* (medicine and a cold handkerchief) *How did the lion help Lara? Where did it take her?* (to the top of the mountain) In L1, discuss the importance of helping each other when a friend is in difficulty or worrying about something. Ask *Can you remember when a friend helped you? How did they help you? How did you feel? How do you feel after you help someone / an animal?* Accept answers in English or L1.

A Read and complete the sentences.

- Review/Teach *alone*. To help understanding, write *alone* on the board. Cross out *al* so learners can see the word *one* and explain that when a person is *alone*, there is only *one* person! Ask one learner to read out the completed example.
- Ask *How many words are there above the sentences?* (eight) *How many sentences are there?* (six) *Do you need to use all the words?* (no) *Now you complete the other sentences.*
- Learners work on their own to write the correct words in the gaps. They compare answers with a partner. Then check answers in open class.
- Ask *What does 'so' mean in sentence 5?* (very/really) Point to different learners and say *You are so clever / kind / good at English!*
- Say *People take medicine when they are …* (sick/ill) *Where do you go to have an x-ray?* (to a hospital) *How do you feel when you have a temperature?* (hot) *Do you like being in dark places? Do you like being alone?*

Answers

2 medicine	**3** x-ray	**4** temperature	**5** dark	**6** sore

B Put the sentences in order. Write numbers.

- Learners read the six sentences.
- Ask *Why is number 1 in the box?* (because that's the first part of the story) Say *Number 1 is in that box because, in the <u>first</u> part of the story, George visited …* (Lara's office)
- Say *Now you write the numbers.* In pairs, learners talk together about the order and write numbers *2–6* in the boxes next to the other five sentences.
- Divide learners into groups of three or four. Groups read aloud the sentences in Activity B and then add, in the correct place, two or three more sentences about the story, e.g. *Lara rode on the lion's back. It was wonderful.* Stronger groups can also copy the six sentences in their notebooks and add extra information, e.g. *Lara rode on the lion's back to the top of the mountain. Lara stayed with her cousins in the winter holidays.*
- Each group tells their version of the story to the class.

Answers

Lara rode on the lion's back. 5
A lion came and spoke to Lara. 4
Lara felt very tired on the mountain. 3
Lara stayed with her cousins. 2
Lara decided to be a vet. 6

Extension

Learners guess what happens to George next. Ask *What next? Does George want to be a vet one day?* (yes) *What animals does he enjoy looking after? Does he have any unusual pets? What are they?* Learners suggest answers.

C Who said this? Write A, B or C.

- Learners look at the pictures and then at the example. Ask *Why is the answer C?* (because George said this)
- In pairs or on their own, learners write *A, B* or *C* on the dotted lines. If necessary, they can find the answers in the story.
- Check the answers in open class. Ask learners to read the sentence in the voice of Lara, George or the mountain lion.

Answers

2 A	**3** C	**4** B	**5** A	**6** B

Extension

Learners find or remember three other sentences from the story, spoken by the boy, the lion and Lara. They write them in their notebooks, in speech bubbles. Learners then swap speech bubbles with a partner, who guesses who said each one.

D Tick (✔) the four best ways to answer the question.

- Learners look at the speech bubbles. Ask *How many do you need to tick?* (four) Point to the orange speech bubble and ask *Who asked this question in the story?* (the mountain lion) In pairs, learners look at the speech bubbles and tick the four appropriate answers to the lion's question.
- Ask *Why are B, D and F not good answers?* Accept reasons in English or in L1.

Answers

A, C, E, G

- Write the following situations on the board. Divide the class into A, B and C groups. Each group discusses their situation. Ask *How can you help these people?*

  A: You are cycling down the road and see an old woman who wants to cross.

  B: You are skateboarding with a friend in the park when your friend falls over and hurts her knee badly.

  C: Your friend is feeling frightened about starting a new school.

- The groups take turns to report back their suggestions to the class.

Extension

Write on the board:
A: *Hi! Are you all right?*
B:
A:
B:
A:
B: *Thank you so much!*
In small groups, learners think of ways to complete the mini-play about helping each other. They write the sentences in their notebooks. Walk around and help with vocabulary and ideas if necessary. When they have finished, two learners from each group perform their mini-play in front of the class.

E   Listen and write about Lara.

- With books closed, ask learners *What can you remember about Lara? What does she look like? Is her office in the countryside or in a city?* Learners tell you as much information as they can, without looking at the story pictures.

- Learners open their books and look at the form in Activity E. Ask *Can you guess these answers? What do you think? What's her favourite animal? When doesn't she work? Why does she enjoy her job? What's her favourite sport?* Learners suggest answers. Say *Now let's listen and write about Lara. Write one word.*

17

- Play the audio twice.

- Check answers in open class. Say *You guessed some of these answers. Were any of your guesses correct?*

- Ask *Does Lara like kittens best?* (no) *Does she often work on Saturdays and Sundays?* (yes)

Answers

tortoises   Wednesday   interesting   snowboarding

Tapescript:

George:	Where did you study to be a vet, Lara?
Lara:	You have to go to university to do that.
George:	Which university did you go to?
Lara:	Castle University. You spell that C-A-S-T-L-E.

Can you see the example? Now you listen and write.

George:	Do you have a favourite kind of animal?
Lara:	I shouldn't have, but yes, I do!
George:	Let me guess ... Kittens?
Lara:	No – tortoises! Their shells are so beautiful and tortoises have such funny, old faces!
George:	Do you have to work every day?

Lara:	Not always. I don't usually work on Wednesdays.
George:	Sorry? You don't usually work on Wednesdays?
Lara:	That's right! But I often have to work on Saturdays and Sundays.
George:	What do you like most about being a vet?
Lara:	That's a good question.
George:	Is it?
Lara:	Yes! I think I like it because it's interesting. Yes, because it's interesting.
George:	And what's your favourite sport, Lara?
Lara:	I love snowboarding! I go snowboarding for two weeks each year.
George:	Wow! You're lucky.
Lara:	I know. Your mum loved that too when she was young.
George:	I didn't know that.

Test tip: FLYERS
Listening (Part 2)

- ✔ Learners may have to write a name of, e.g. a school, street or town in their form. The name is usually less than eight letters long. If the word is not on the Starters, Movers or Flyers word list, it is spelled out.
- → Give learners practice in both spelling and writing spellings correctly. Learners could make up names, e.g. of an imagined friend, the city they live in and a sports centre they go to, and write these down secretly. They then spell these names out and their partner writes them down. Learners compare spellings.

Extension

In pairs, learners listen to the audio again and then role play the conversation. They could also use the completed form to help them ask and answer the questions.

F   Draw lines. Make sentences.

- Say *Lara stayed with her cousins in the holidays because she didn't have any ...* (brothers or sisters to play with.) Write on the board: *Lara stayed with her cousins in the holidays because she had no brothers or sisters to play with.* Underline *because*.

- Say *Now look at the example here. Lara had no brothers or sisters, so ...* (she stayed with her cousins in the holidays.) Write this answer on the board and underline *so*. Ask *Does 'so' mean 'very' or 'really' here?* (no)

- Explain in L1 that *because* introduces the reason for an action and *so* introduces the action that is the result of something. An action that is the result of something comes <u>after</u> *so* or <u>before</u> *because*. Say *I'm good at basketball. Why? Because I'm really tall. I'm really tall, so I'm good at basketball.*

- Learners could look at page 44 and underline the three examples of *so* in the second and fourth paragraphs.

- In pairs, learners match and join the half sentences with *so*. The story information is on page 44.

- Check answers by asking different pairs to read out one of the completed sentences.

Extension

Write the following sentences on the board. Learners choose three of these and copy them in their notebooks. They then complete the sentences with their own ideas for homework.

I didn't feel well last Saturday, so …
A mountain lion was behind me, so …
My baby brother's got a toothache, so …
I saw a bear in that cave, so …
My grandpa had a headache, so …
I love helping animals, so …

G Which are the lion's answers? Write A–F.

- Learners look at the picture. Ask *Where are Lara and the lion?* (on the mountain) *What time of year is it, do you think?* (winter) *What's Lara wearing?* (a hat, a jacket, a scarf, some jeans) *What's behind Lara and the lion?* (the mountains, the forest, some snow, some rocks) *What's in front of Lara and the lion? It's keeping them warm!* (a fire) Explain that the speech bubbles show different things that Lara said.

- Write on the board:
  What did Lara hurt?
  Why is it difficult for Lara to walk?
  How is she feeling?

- In pairs, learners choose their own answers to these questions. They can use some information in Lara's speech bubbles to answer them. Learners write their answers in their notebooks, e.g. *Lara hurt her hand and her elbow. She was tired. She is cold and hungry.*

- Ask different pairs to tell their answers to the class.

- Learners look at the example. Ask two learners to read Lara's sentence and the lion's answer (B). Say *Read the other four things that Lara said. What does the lion say? Write A, C, D, E or F.*

- Check answers by asking five different pairs to role play the exchanges.

Answers

E, C, A, D

H What did Lara do each day? Listen and write a letter in each box.

- Ask *Do you ever go to the mountains? What did you do there?* Use photographs on the Image carousel to review/teach *skiing, sledging, skating* and *ice hockey.* Ask *What else can you do in the snow?* (walk, make snowmen, throw snowballs)

- Say *Listen. Lara is talking to her father on the telephone. She is talking about things she did with the mountain lion. What did Lara do each day?*

- Learners look at pictures A–F. Ask *How many pictures are there?* (six) *How many days can you see?* (five) Say *One of the pictures is not a correct answer.*

18

- Play the audio and pause after the example. Ask *What did Lara do on Monday?* (she rode on the back of a mountain lion) *Which picture shows this?* (C)

- Learners listen to Lara and her father and write a letter in each box. Play the recording a second time.

- Check answers in open class.

Answers

Tuesday A   Wednesday B   Thursday E   Friday D

Tapescript:

Lara:	Hi, Dad! I'm having a wonderful holiday here in the mountains!
Dad:	Great!
Lara:	On Monday I went for a ride on the back of a mountain lion after I gave it some medicine! It wasn't very well, you see …
Dad:	Oh dear!

Can you see the letter C? Now you listen and write a letter in each box.

Dad:	What else did you do this week?
Lara:	Well, on Wednesday I went ice skating.
Dad:	Yes …?
Lara:	I only fell over a few times, so that was OK.
Dad:	I'm pleased to hear that!
Lara:	And after lunch on Thursday, I had a skiing lesson.
Dad:	Did you enjoy that?
Lara:	Yes! It was amazing! I had such a lot of fun. I'm not very good at it, so I had to go very slowly. Can I have some more skiing lessons next year?
Dad:	Sure!
Dad:	Did you see the ice hockey game on Tuesday?
Lara:	No. We couldn't drive there because it snowed too much. But it was good because I played with some other children here instead.
Dad:	Did you throw snowballs?
Lara:	Yes! I got very wet and cold, but it was all right. We had a drink of hot chocolate before we went back to the hotel again.
Dad:	Good idea!
Dad:	What did you do on Friday?
Lara:	We pulled the sledges up the hill and played on them all morning. I was very tired after we did that.
Dad:	And how are you now, Lara?
Lara:	I'm fine. I've got a toothache, but I've got my medicine too. Don't worry!
Dad:	OK!

✔ In the second set of pictures, five will match correctly and two will not be needed, but all seven will be heard in the conversation. The set of possible answers might be different places, activities, possessions, etc. The pictures usually feature Flyers vocabulary.

→ Play 'Where?' guessing games to revise vocabulary sets. A learner chooses secretly where they 'work' in town. Other learners guess the place by asking *Do you work in/at the …?*

Make sure learners know all the Flyers places in town: *airport, bank, bridge, chemist, club, college, factory, fire station, hotel, museum, police station, post office, restaurant, skyscraper, stadium, theatre, university.*

Extension

Ask *What did Lara tell her father about her day?* Write short sentences on the board, e.g.
It snowed.
Lara went to the village.
Children were throwing snowballs.
Lara got wet and cold.
Lara and her cousins had a drink of hot chocolate.
They went home again.
Learners copy these sentences and use them to write a short story about Lara's day for homework. They make longer sentences by adding *so, because, before* or *after* and they can add other ideas to make the story more exciting. They can then tell their story in groups.

Listen and write the words.

• Ask learners if they can remember the six things that Lara and the mountain lion talked about in the story. If they can't remember, they can find the answers on page 45. (X-rays and Saturdays, bandages and jam sandwiches, temperatures and school teachers) Show learners that the endings of these paired words sound the same.

• Write on the board:
cave   hair   snake   no

• Check learners understand the meaning of *cave*.

• In pairs, learners try to think of other words that sound like these, e.g.

cave:	*brave, gave, wave*
hair:	*bear, air, pear, stair, wear*
snake:	*make, take, wake, cake*
no:	*go, grow, low, know, show, throw, so*

• Learners look at the picture. Ask *Which three animals can you see?* (a lion, a monster, a snake) *Which is very furry?* (the monster) *Which wants something to eat?* (the snake) *Which is in a cave?* (the lion)

• Learners look at the poem. Say *Some of the words at the ends of the lines sound the same too.*

19
• Play the audio. Learners listen and write the words.

• Learners compare answers and listen again to check.

Answers

2 brave **3** behind **4** air **5** ask **6** cake **7** story
8 know

Tapescript:

See SB page 51 and Answers above.

6

Let's have fun!

Design a special home for two mountain lion cubs.

Learners look at page 70, Activity 6. Learners read about the project. Explain that very young lions are called *cubs*. Ask *What do you have to design?* (a home) *What is it for?* (two mountain lion cubs) *Think about what lions need.*

In small groups, learners use the questions to discuss their ideas. Give each group a large sheet of paper. They can draw the lion cubs' special home and write a description.

If possible, display the designs on a classroom wall.

6

Let's speak!

Talk about jobs.

Provide the following prompts on the board:
What job would/wouldn't you like to do? Why?
a vet, a pop star, a doctor, an engineer, an astronaut, a designer, a fire fighter, a journalist, a pilot, a dentist, a police officer, a photographer, a film star, an actor

Learners look at page 73, Activity 6. Point to the prompts on the board. Ask two or three confident pairs to role play the mini-conversation using words on the board or their own ideas.

Give each learner Photocopy 6 (TB page 59).

Learners look at the different people doing their jobs. Review/Teach any jobs they are not sure of.

Learners write the jobs under each picture.

In groups of three or four, learners decide which three jobs are the best. They give three points to their favourite job, two to the second best, and one to their third choice. Ask groups for their scores to find the most popular job in the class.

Ask *What did the boy in the story want to be?* (a vet) *Is that a good job? Why?* Listen to learners' ideas.

Answers

artist	teacher	dentist	waiter
pilot	farmer	cook	journalist
designer	film star	nurse	doctor
taxi driver	pop star	astronaut	actor
fire fighter	mechanic	police officer	photographer

29
Let's say! Page 75

Say *Look at page 75, Activity 6. Listen.* Play the audio. Say *Let's say /w/. Quick, question, why, wash, wild, whale, when, well.* Learners repeat.
Say *Tell me more English words with /w/.* Learners answer (e.g. water, white, walk). Learners listen again to the audio, repeating the rhyme as fast as they can.

Home FUN booklet

➥ **Pages 16–17, health**
➥ **Picture dictionary: health**

Go online

to practise your English
to listen to the audio recordings
to find more FUN activities!

Harry's diary

7

Main topics:	home, time
Story summary:	Harry writes his diary entry for the day.
Main grammar:	past continuous, *still* and *already*, taste, smell, sound, feel, look like + noun phrase
Main vocabulary:	*at the moment, biscuit, borrow, cereal, comb, drums, expensive, forget, frightened, gold, high, hurry, key, lovely, minute, newspaper, octopus, program, puzzle, salt, secret, shampoo, sound, spaceship, spoon, sugar, take (time), timetable, tomorrow, turn on, whisper, wi-fi*
Value:	Being forgiving (*"Never mind!"*)
Let's say!:	/j/
Practice for Flyers:	Reading and Writing Part 1 (A), Reading and Writing Part 4 (E), Listening Part 4 (F), Speaking Part 3 (G), Speaking Part 1 (I), Speaking Part 4 (Let's speak!)
Equipment:	• ▶ audio: Storytelling, F, Let's say! • ➡ ⟮presentation **PLUS**⟯ flashcards Go to Presentation plus to find pictures of Flyers vocabulary from Unit 7. You can use the pictures to teach/review important words in this unit.	• ➡ ⟮presentation **PLUS**⟯ Image carousel 49–61 (cereal, coffee, glue, key, salt, scissors, spoon, sugar, ticket, lamp, laptop, memory stick, phone case): Storytelling, I • crayons or colouring pencils: A, Let's have fun! • Photocopy 7, one per learner (TB page 60): Let's have fun!

 Storytelling

Before listening

With books closed …

- Introduce the topic of the story. Ask *Do you have a diary? How often do you write in your diary? What do you write about? What's the difference between a diary and a calendar?*

- Review/Teach *salt, sugar, coffee, cereal, spoon, ticket, key, glue* and *scissors*, using the Image carousel. Remember you can use the flashcards on Presentation plus to help you teach and review vocabulary.

- Say *This story is about a funny Tuesday. A boy wrote about it in his diary. What do you do on Tuesdays? What must you do before you go to school?* Whisper to three different learners to mime washing their face, cleaning their teeth and combing their hair and ask *What are they doing?*

- Ask *Which subjects do you study at school?* Learners list the school subjects they know in English. Write them on the board. Elicit *English, art, maths, music, history, geography, information technology, gym/PE* and *science*, translating into L1 if necessary. Ask *Which school subjects do you do on Tuesdays?*

- Look at the first story picture of the boy's face without the story text on the Image carousel or with the story text in the book on page 52. Say *This is Harry, the boy who wrote about a funny Tuesday in his diary.*

- Say *Tell me more about Harry. Guess! How old is he? What does he like doing? Has he got any brothers and sisters? Has he got a pet? What does he like eating? Is he kind, funny, brave, friendly? Let's find out.*

- Say *Now let's listen to the story.* Say *Let's look at page 52. Let's read Harry's diary and check.*

Listening

With books open …

20

- Play the audio or read the story. Learners listen.

- Play the audio or read the story again.

- Pause after *She put a biscuit in the hole where the CDs went!* on page 53. Ask *How many sisters has Harry got?* (two) *What are they called?* (Sarah and Holly) *What did Harry's dad put in his coffee instead of sugar?* (salt) *What colour is Harry's school shirt now?* (pink) *Why? What did his mum wash it with?* (Harry's red football socks) *What does the new school bus driver have in his mouth?* (three gold teeth)

- Pause again after *She said, 'Well, you needed a wash'* on page 55. Ask *Whose rucksack did Harry pick up?* (Emma's) *Where did Harry kick the football?* (onto the roof) *What did Harry find on the roof?* (three more footballs) *Why did he have to walk home?* (he missed the bus)

- After listening to the whole story, ask *What's Harry doing now?* (going to sleep) *What's in his bed?* (a biscuit)

After listening

- Ask *What does Harry like doing?* (playing volleyball, playing football, chatting with his friends, inventing things, playing the drums) *Do you like doing those things? What does Harry like eating?* (chocolate and chips) *Does Harry like his sisters?* (learners give their opinions)
- Ask *Is Harry a good brother? Is he a good friend? What do you think of Harry?* (learners give their opinions)

 Value

- In L1, discuss Harry's attitude to things that go wrong. Ask *Does he get angry? Is he worried? Does he feel sad?* (no) *Harry understands that sometimes things go wrong but says 'Never mind'.* Explain that we can say *Never mind* when we want to show that we are not angry or upset about something bad that has happened. Ask *When did you, or someone you know, break something that was important to you? How did you feel when that happened? How do you feel about that now?*

 A Complete the crossword.

- Learners look at the puzzle. Say *Three words are already here. Which is a kind of book?* (a dictionary) *And something you use to eat with?* (a spoon) *Now look carefully at the numbers and write the answers in the squares that go down the puzzle.* Learners work on their own or in pairs to complete the crossword.
- Check answers in open class, asking *How do you spell that?* for each word.

Answers

1 salt   2 octopus   3 maths   4 pyjamas   5 drum
6 cereal

Extension

Play a vocabulary drawing game. In groups of four or six, learners form two teams. A team member chooses one of the words from the crossword (or a word from another part of the story) and has one minute to draw it for other learners in their team to guess. They shouldn't give any clues. If they guess correctly, the team scores a point. Then it is the next team's turn to draw and guess.

 B Write *before* or *after*.

- Ask *Which sport did Harry play first? Volleyball or football?* (volleyball) Say *Yes, Harry played volleyball before he played football.* Write the sentence on the board. Then write:

  Harry played football _____ he played volleyball.

- Point to the gap. Ask *What can we write here?* (after) Say *Yes. Harry played football after he played volleyball.* Complete the sentence with *after*.
- Say *We can use 'before' or 'after' to join two sentences together.*
- Learners look at the example in Activity B. Ask *When did Harry have dinner?* (before the wi-fi stopped working) *How can we use 'after' in this sentence instead?* (The wi-fi stopped working after Harry had dinner.)
- Learners work in pairs to complete the sentences from memory. When they finish, they can check their answers in the story.
- Check answers in open class. With stronger learners, ask *How can you say that another way?* (Learners reverse the sentence order and replace *before* with *after*, or vice versa.)

Answers

2 after   3 before   4 after   5 after   6 before

Extension

In pairs, learners write two more *after/before* gapped sentences about the story for other pairs to complete.

 C Tick (✔) three things Harry talked to William and Emma about.

- Ask *What are Harry's friends called?* (William and Emma) Say *Look at the pictures. What can you see?* (shampoo, a cup (of coffee) and a spoon, a computer, a dinosaur, socks) *Which three things did Harry talk to William and Emma about?* Learners tick the boxes. They can check in the story to find their answers.
- Say *So we don't tick the cup or the dinosaur.* Ask *Who made a mistake and put salt in a cup of coffee?* (Harry's dad) *Where was the dinosaur project?* (in Emma's bag)
- Ask *What do you talk to your friends about? What do you often talk about? What do you sometimes/never/always talk about?*
- Review/Teach the different Flyers verbs we can use to mean the same as *talk*: *chat, speak, whisper.* Learners circle all the 'talking' verbs in the story. They will also find *say, tell* and *ask* in Harry's diary.

Answers

shampoo, computer program, socks that smell like flowers

 D What are these people thinking? You decide. Look and write.

- Say *Look at the pictures. What can you see?* (Harry in his pink school shirt, a girl looking at the rain, a girl looking for a key) Say *All the pictures show a problem. What's the problem?* (Harry's shirt was white, but now it's pink. The girl can't go outside. The girl can't open the door.) Say *Now write the sentences. What are they thinking?* Learners work in small groups to think of ideas and choose what to complete the two empty speech bubbles with, e.g. *... make some cookies / watch a movie / draw some cartoons. ... call Mum / climb in a window / go to a friend's house.*
- Walk around and help with vocabulary if necessary. When they finish, groups take turns to read out their completed thought bubbles in open class.

Read and circle the correct answer.

- Say *Listen and write.* Dictate these sentences to learners, to write in their notebooks:

  Dad was coughing a lot when I ran downstairs.

  When I was chatting, I put my rucksack down next to theirs.

  When we were playing football, I kicked the ball so high it went up onto the roof.

- Say *Now find and underline these three sentences in Harry's diary.* Give learners time to check their own dictations.

- Ask *When Harry ran downstairs, what was his dad doing?* (he was coughing) *When Harry put his rucksack down, what was Harry doing with his friends?* (he was chatting) *When Harry kicked the ball really high, what game was Harry playing?* (he was playing football)

- Write on the board *Dad was coughing. I was chatting. We were playing.* Point out the *-ing* ending on the main verb. In L1, explain that these sentences are in the past continuous tense. We use the past continuous to talk about something that was happening when something else suddenly happened. *What suddenly happened in the first sentence?* (Harry ran downstairs) *What suddenly happened in the last sentence?* (Harry kicked the ball on the roof) *What tense do we use for the sudden action?* (past simple)

- Learners look at Activity E and the example. Say *Find the past continuous tense in the example* (he was doing). *Find the past simple tense in the example* (Emma phoned Harry).

- Say *Now choose the right words. Think – is it present simple, past simple or past continuous?*

- Learners work on their own or in pairs to complete the task. Check answers in open class.

Answers

2 made **3** designing **4** play **5** works **6** looking

Extension

Write on the board:
When I was _____ ing _____,
_____ !
Complete the structure with some funny examples:
When I was having a bath, a fish jumped out of the water!
When I was cycling to school, an eagle flew in front of me!
Say *Write two more crazy sentences about something that suddenly happened.* In pairs, learners write more sentences, following the same structure.
Walk around and help with grammar and vocabulary if necessary.
Pairs take turns to report back their sentences in open class. Ask *Which is the funniest sentence?*

Listen and tick (✔) the box.

- Say *Look at the 12 pictures. What can you see?* Learners talk about the pictures in pairs.

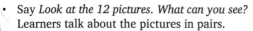

- Say *Listen and tick the box, A, B or C, that shows the right answer to each question.* Learners read questions 1–4 before listening.

21

- Play the audio. Pause after number 1 to check learners have ticked the right answer. Ask *What is Harry eating now?* (cereal) *What was he eating before?* (bread and jam) *When can he eat a chocolate biscuit?*

(in his break) and then play the whole audio twice.

- Learners compare their answers in pairs. Check answers in open class, asking the questions: *What's in Harry's pocket?* (a comb), etc.

Answers

1 A **2** B **3** C **4** B

Tapescript:

1 What is Harry eating now?

  Dad: Are you still eating that bread and jam, Harry?

  Harry: No, Dad. I found the new box of cereal. I'm eating some of that now.

  Dad: OK. Well, be quick! And take a chocolate biscuit to eat in your break.

  Harry: All right. Thanks.

2 What is in Harry's pocket?

  Mum: Make sure your pockets are empty before I wash your jeans, Harry.

  Harry: OK. I haven't got any money in them.

  Mum: Look again.

  Harry: All right ... Oh! My comb's still here!

  Mum: Right. Take it out. And what about your key? Where's that?

  Harry: That's in my school bag, Mum.

3 What is Harry drawing now?

  Harry: I'm still drawing your favourite animal, Holly. Look!

  Holly: A dinosaur?

  Harry: Well done! Would you like me to draw an octopus too?

  Holly: No. An eagle.

  Harry: OK. In a minute.

4 What is Harry studying?

  Emma: What are you studying, Harry? Is that your information technology work?

  Harry: No. And I still can't find the answers for our geography homework ...

  Emma: So you're reading something to help with your science project?

  Harry: That's right.

Test tip: FLYERS
Listening (Part 4)

✔ Learners listen to a conversation and choose the correct picture (of three) that shows the right answer to a question. It is important that they read the question carefully before they look at the pictures and check the three possible answers.

→ Show learners typical Part 4 picture sets, e.g. a skyscraper, a factory, a bridge. In pairs, learners think up three or four alternative questions that the picture set might answer, e.g. *Where is Henry now? Where does Henry's dad work? Which place does Henry want to visit? What is in Henry's picture?* Pairs then choose a question and write one turn of a conversation that includes their choice of answer.

G Look at the pictures and tell the story.

- Say *Look at the pictures. What can you see?* Give learners a few minutes to look at the pictures and talk to each other about what's happening. Then point to each picture and ask:

  In picture one: What's Harry doing? What is watching him? Is the dog dirty or clean?

  In picture two: Where's Harry now? What's he doing?

  In picture three: Is Harry's dog clean or dirty now? What does the dog smell like?

Test tip: FLYERS
Speaking (Part 3)

- ✔ Learners look at a cartoon strip of five pictures and tell its story. Some learners find this task quite challenging, but train them to just look at one picture at a time and to think of just two or three things to say about what is happening in that picture.
- → Show learners any single picture and ask easy questions about what they can see, e.g. *How many people are in this forest? What are the children doing? What kind of animal is behind that tree?*

Extension

Write the questions you asked about the three pictures on the board. Learners use full sentence answers to write the story in their notebooks (in order to practise Flyers Reading and Writing Part 7).

Suggested answers

Harry is making some banana shampoo. His dog is watching. His dog is dirty!
Harry is in the garden. He's washing his dog.
The dog is clean now! It smells like bananas!

H Complete the sentences with your own words.

- Review/Teach *smell like, taste like, sound like* and *look like*. Say *You're inventing a soap with a special smell. What do you want it to smell like? You're inventing a toothpaste with a special taste. What does it taste like? You're camping in the woods and hear a strange noise outside your tent. What does it sound like?* Ask *Who do you look like? Someone else in your family?* Say *When I sing, I sound like* [a famous singer known to your learners]. *Who do you sound like?*
- Learners look at Activity H. Say *You can choose words to complete the sentences.*
- Learners work on their own to complete the sentences. In small groups, learners read out their sentences and talk about their answers. Groups take turns to read out the most interesting sentences to the rest of the class.

Extension

Ask *What do you think of Harry's ideas for inventions?* In small groups, learners talk about their ideas for inventions.
For support you could draw this table on the board:

1	that tastes like	
2	that smells like	
3	that sounds like	
4	that feels like	
5	that looks like	

Learners choose ways to complete the first and third columns, e.g.
1 a fruit / chocolate **2** a car / toothpaste
3 a phone / a bee **4** a scarf / fur **5** a bed / a spaceship
Groups use their own ideas to write a list of inventions. Groups report back to the class. Ask the class to vote for the funniest idea and the most helpful idea. Learners can write about, illustrate and label their favourite invention idea in their notebooks for homework.

I Look at the pictures. Find six differences.

- Review/Teach *lamp, laptop, mouse mat, memory stick, phone case.* Use photographs from the Image carousel (or real items) and a real mouse mat. Remember you can also use the flashcards on Presentation plus to help you teach and review vocabulary.
- Say *Look at Harry's desk. How is William's desk different?*
- Write on the board:

  In this picture, ..., but in this picture, ...
- Point to the structure and ask one learner to complete the sentence about one difference.
- Say *Now find and talk about six differences.* Learners work in pairs to describe the differences.
- Check answers in open class.

Answers

Learners find six of the following:
In this picture, the mouse mat is blue, but in this picture, it is red.
In this picture, the time is 11.13, but in this picture, it is 12.11.
In this picture, there are two memory sticks, but in this picture, there is one.
In this picture, the lamp is silver, but in this picture, it is gold.
In this picture, the phone case is closed, but in this picture, it is open.
In this picture, there is a beetle on the laptop, but in this picture, there is a tortoise.
In this picture, the pen is in front of the lamp, but in this picture, the pen is in front of the clock.
In this picture, there is a ruler, but in this picture, there is no ruler.

7 *Let's have fun!*

Invent a new drink.

Learners look at page 71, Activity 7. They look at the picture and read the bullets. Ask *What do you have to do?* (invent a new drink) Read aloud the questions together, asking for ideas in open class: *What does it taste like?* (Oranges! Chocolate! Coffee!)

Give each learner Photocopy 7 (TB page 60). Learners design an advert for their new drink and give it a name and a price. They write a description, answering the questions on page 71.

7 Let's speak!

Talk about your day.

Learners look at page 73, Activity 7. Ask four learners to read out the questions. Ask different learners *What about you? What time do you get up? What do you do after school?*

Learners talk about their day in pairs or small groups. Walk around and help with vocabulary if necessary. Learners tell the class about one of their own or their partner's answers.

30

)) Let's say! Page 75

Say *Look at page 75, Activity 7. Listen.* Play the audio. Say *Let's say /j/. Used, onions, huge, yoghurt, yesterday.* Say *Tell me more English words with /j/.* Learners answer (e.g. yellow, view, cute).
Learners listen again to the audio, repeating the rhyme as fast as they can.

Home FUN booklet

➡ Pages 18–19, school
➡ Picture dictionary: the home, school

Go online

to practise your English
to listen to the audio recordings
to find more FUN activities!

Summer fun

8

Main topics:	friends, jobs
Story summary:	Katy, Helen, Frank and Dan are very different. This is a play about how they spend a summer day in the garden.
Main grammar:	*as … as, going to*
Main vocabulary:	*actually, artist, dangerous, designer, dinosaur, exciting, gate, high, important, large, manager, mechanic, missing, noisy, photographer, pond, queen, racing (car), stream, study, turn off, whistle, wild*
Value:	Asking for help when you need it (*"Thanks for your help!"*)
Let's say!:	/z/
Practice for Flyers:	Reading and Writing Part 1 (A), Reading and Writing Part 2 (D), Reading and Writing Part 5 (F), Listening Part 5 (G), Speaking Part 2 (H), Speaking Part 4 (Let's speak!)

Equipment:	
• ▶ audio: Storytelling, G, Let's say! • ↪ (presentation **PLUS**) flashcards Go to Presentation plus to find pictures of Flyers vocabulary from Unit 8. You can use the pictures to teach/review important words in this unit.	• ↪ (presentation **PLUS**) Image carousel 62–74 (actor, designer, journalist, manager, mechanic, photographer, queen; flag, gate, glove, newspaper, umbrella; key): A, G, G Extension • props for the play (optional): box of crayons, a mobile phone, a pad of paper, a (plastic) bunch of grapes: Let's have fun! • crayons or colouring pencils: G, Let's have fun! • Photocopy 8, one per learner (TB page 61): Let's have fun!

Storytelling

Before listening

With books closed …

- Introduce the story by talking about plays. Review/Teach *play*. Ask *Where can you see a play?* (at the theatre) *Can you think of any famous plays?* (e.g. Romeo and Juliet) *What do you see in a play?* Learners brainstorm associated vocabulary, e.g. *actors, costumes, a stage*. Write the words on the board. Remember you can use the flashcards on Presentation plus to help you teach and review vocabulary.
- Say *This a play about four friends who live in South America.* Review/Teach *iguanas, foxes, eagles* and *dinosaurs*. Ask *Which animals might live in South America?* (iguanas, foxes and eagles) *And dinosaurs? Where do they live?* Learners answer.
- Look at the first story picture without the story text on the Image carousel or with the story text in the book on page 60. Ask *How many friends can you see?* (two) *What are they looking at?* (a text message, a tree)
- Say *Now let's listen to the play.* Say *Let's look at page 60.*

Listening

With books open …

▶ Play the audio or read the play. Learners listen.
Play the audio or ask learners to read the play.

22
- Pause at the end of Scene 1 on page 60. Ask *What is Katy doing on her phone?* (sending a message) *Why?* (someone needs help) *What does Helen want to climb?* (a tall tree) *How many questions is Helen thinking about?* (four) *Which animals does Helen want to draw?* (iguanas, eagles, foxes or dinosaurs) *What does Helen borrow?* (some crayons)
- Pause at the end of Scene 2 on page 62. Review/Teach *racing car* and *quad bike*. Ask *What are Helen's four questions?* (Why don't people let children drive racing cars? Why do kids have to go to school? Why are mangoes more orange inside than oranges? Why can't you buy cat food that tastes like mice?) *Can you answer her questions?* Learners suggest answers. Review/Teach *chase*. Ask *Who is chasing Frank and Dan?* (Mr Whistle and the wild white horse) *What is Mr Whistle riding on?* (his quad bike)
- After listening to the whole story, ask *Why was Mr Whistle angry?* (because Dan took some grapes) *Who was Katy sending messages to?* (Frank)

After listening

- Ask *Where are the children going to go now?* (to the stream) *Why?* (to look for animals)

A Read and write the word.

- Use the Image carousel to teach *manager, queen, journalist, actor, designer, photographer* and *mechanic*. Ask *Who fixes cars?* (a mechanic) *Who works on a stage?* (an actor) *Who needs a camera?* (a photographer) *Who might wear a crown?* (a queen)

- Learners look at the 'job' words, the sentences and the example in Activity A. Ask *Who wears a crown on her head?* (a queen) Ask *Are there the same number of words and sentences?* (no) Say *There are two extra jobs.*

- Learners choose answers on their own and then compare them in pairs.

- Check answers in open class by asking questions: *Who paints or draws pictures?* (an artist) *Who fixes cars?* (a mechanic) *Who is good at taking photos?* (a photographer) *In a business, who might have lots of people working for them?* (a manager) *Who writes stories for a newspaper?* (a journalist)

- Ask *Which two jobs weren't answers?* (an actor, a designer) In open class, write clues for these jobs:

  This person might wear a costume and work on TV, in a theatre or in films.

  This person might draw and make things like clothes, games, toys or things for the home.

- Ask *Which job or jobs would you like to do? Why?*

Answers

2 an artist   **3** a mechanic   **4** a photographer
5 a manager   **6** a journalist

Extension

Say *Make a list of all the jobs you know.* In pairs, learners write a list in their notebooks. Give a few examples, e.g. *teacher, farmer.*
After a few minutes, ask each pair to choose a word from their list, in secret. The rest of the class ask questions to guess the job, e.g.
Do you wear a uniform?
Do you work outside?
Do you work on a computer?
Do you work with animals?
Do you work in an office / a shop / a school?
Is your job dangerous/difficult/unusual?
The pair can only say *yes* or *no.* Continue until all pairs have had a turn.

B Read the questions. Draw lines to the right person.

- Ask *What are the children called in the story?* (Katy, Helen, Dan and Frank) *Who are cousins?* (Katy and Helen) *Who is the kindest person in the story?* (Katy) *Why do you think that?* (Learners suggest ideas, e.g. Katy helps Frank. Katy lets Helen borrow her crayons.) *Who loves doing exciting things?* (Helen and Dan)

- Learners look at the example in Activity B. Say *Why does the line go from sentence 1 to Katy?* (because Katy sent a secret message)

- Learners work on their own or in pairs to draw lines between each question and its answer. They can check their answers in the story when they finish.

Answers

2 Katy   **3** Dan   **4** Mr Whistle   **5** Dan   **6** Frank   **7** Helen

Extension

In pairs, learners write two more *Who* questions about the play in their notebooks for other pairs to answer.

C Complete the sentences with your own words.

- In L1, explain how to use *(not) as* + adjective + *as* to compare things. Choose two learners to come to the front of the class. They should share a characteristic and also be different in some way. Say how they are the same, e.g. *Maria is as kind as Anna. They are both kind. Maria isn't kinder than Anna and Anna isn't kinder than Maria.* Say (sensitively) how they are different, e.g. *But Maria is not as tall as Anna. Maria is shorter. Anna is taller than Maria.*

- Learners look at the example. Say *Now you complete the sentences. You choose the words.* Learners work on their own, and then compare their ideas in small groups. Ask each group to feed back a few sentences in open class.

Suggested answers

2 brave   **3** funny   **4** happy   **5** clever   **6** naughty
7 big   **8** scary

D Choose the best answer. Write a letter A–G.

- Learners look at Frank's first question. Ask *Which letter shows Dan's answer?* (E) Learners cover the answers A–G. Say *Let's guess Dan's other answers now.* Learners look at 2–5 and suggest answers, e.g. *2 Because I'm hungry. 3 In the field. 4 A box. 5 Yes!*

- Say *Now read answers A–G and find the answers. Be careful! Two of these are not answers to any of the questions.* Learners work on their own or in pairs. Check answers in class by asking different learners to read out each exchange.

- Ask *Which answers didn't you use?* (B and F)

Answers

2 G   **3** D   **4** C   **5** A

Extension

Write on the board *What are you going to do now?* If possible, learners get up and walk around the class. Each time they come face to face with a classmate, they stop and take turns to ask and answer the question. Encourage learners to be as adventurous as they like, e.g. *I'm going to swim across the ocean.* Assure them that their answers don't have to be truthful!

E   Asking for help. Which are the three kindest answers?

- Ask *What can you see in the picture?* (a phone / a text message) *What does the message say?* ('I've got a problem!') *What do you think the problem is?* (learners guess)

- Check understanding of *kindest* and then divide learners into small groups. Say *Choose the three answers you think are kindest.* Learners discuss the answers and then feed back in open class.

- Groups talk about the other expressions in the word box. Write on the board:

  A: _____ .

  B: *Never mind!*

- Say *B answers 'Never mind!' What did A say? You choose.* Groups complete four exchanges and read them out to the rest of the class.

- Choose other expressions for B's answer, e.g. *In a minute.* Groups choose A's questions in the same way.

Suggested answers

What's the matter?
How can I help?
Tell me about it.

Test tip: FLYERS
Reading and Writing (Part 2)

✔ Learners may find *Where, Why, Who, When, Whose, What, How often, How long, How many* open questions or *Are, Were, Do, Did, Have,* etc. closed questions before the missing answer gaps. Make sure learners recognise what kinds of answers are likely to follow these.

→ Use pictures to prompt practice for inventing open questions and accept any appropriate answer, e.g. *Where did you find that key?* (on the floor, in the restaurant, in Field Street, in the supermarket car park, under the bridge)

Extension

Do a creative thinking exercise. Ask *How did Katy help Frank? Why didn't Frank want Helen or Dan to know?* Learners talk about the questions in their groups and feed back ideas. Accept any plausible reason, e.g. *Katy is helping Frank to plan a surprise birthday party / make a birthday present for Dan.*

F   Complete the sentences. Write 1, 2, 3 or 4 words. You choose the words.

- Say *Tell me about the picture.* Learners describe what they can see in the lake picture. Ask questions to prompt learners, if necessary, e.g. *Where is this place? What can people do there? What's the weather like? What can you hear? Would you like to visit this place? Why?*

- Review/Teach the future form *going to.* Say *Frank, Dan, Katy and Helen are going to go to the lake Road and complete the sentences. You choose the words. What are they going to do there?*

- Learners work in pairs to write a completed text. Pairs show their text to another pair. Ask different pairs to read out their texts.

Suggested answers

Helen and Katy are going to **go for a ride in a boat** and then Dan is going to **try to catch a fish**. Katy is going to **make a fire on the island** and then Frank and Dan are going to **run up the hill**. After that, the four friends are going to **play on the swing**.

Extension

Learners think about three fun things they are going to do next weekend. These can be real or imagined. They write and illustrate three *going to* sentences in their notebooks for homework.

G   Listen, colour and write.

- With books closed, review/teach *newspaper, umbrella, gate, flag* and *glove,* using photographs on the Image carousel.

- Say *Look at the picture.* Ask *What can you see?* Learners describe the picture. Prompt with questions if necessary: *Who can you see?* (Helen and Katy) *Where are they?* (in a garden) *What are they doing?* (sitting/dancing) *What animals can you see?* (an iguana / a spider)

- Say *A teacher is talking to a girl about this picture. Listen, colour and write.*

23

- Make sure that learners all have crayons or colouring pencils. Play the audio.

- Play the audio a second time. Allow learners time to finish their colouring. Check answers in open class.

Answers

gate – red
newspaper on the step – yellow
glove on Helen's hand – purple
'Sunny' written on the umbrella

Tapescript:

Girl:	This looks interesting! Is it a picture of the two girls before they climbed the tree?
Man:	Yes. Would you like to colour it?
Girl:	OK. Wow! That creature looks like a lizard, but is it an iguana?
Man:	Yes, it is. Colour it green!
Girl:	All right!

Can you see the green lizard? This is an example. Now you listen and colour and write.

1	**Girl:**	What can I colour next?
	Man:	Well, next to the building, there's a little gate. Colour that.
	Girl:	All right. Which colour would you like me to use?
	Man:	Red, please.
	Girl:	Fine! There!

2	Man:	Let's colour the newspaper next.
	Girl:	Do you mean the one on the round table?
	Man:	The other one, actually. The one on the step.
	Girl:	OK. Which is the best colour for that?
	Man:	Yellow. Make it that colour, please.
3	Man:	I'd like you to write something here as well.
	Girl:	Good. I like writing … What shall I write on?
	Man:	The umbrella. Write the word 'Sunny' on it.
	Girl:	Because the weather is often hot here?
	Man:	That's right.
	Girl:	OK. I'm doing that now.
4	Girl:	Anything else? Can I colour Helen's flag?
	Man:	No, but you can colour her glove. Make it purple.
	Girl:	Excellent! … Why is she only wearing one?
	Man:	I don't know! But thanks for making this picture as good as the others now.
	Girl:	That's OK!

Test tip: FLYERS
Listening (Part 5)

✔ Learners need to write two words somewhere in the picture. If a word is from the YLE word list, it will not be spelled out, but the context should make it easy for learners to write the correct word. If the word is a name, e.g. *Keilay (Hotel)*, and not on the word list, it will be spelled out.

➜ Use any picture in the book and tell learners to add an appropriate word or short phrase to the scene.

Extension

Use the picture to play a guessing game. Say *I'm going to hide this key somewhere in the garden.* Hold up a key, or show the photograph of the key from the Image carousel. Say *Can you guess where it is?*
Learners take turns to ask *yes/no* questions until they guess correctly, e.g. *Is it under the table? Is it on the step? Is it in Helen's pocket? Is it in the tree? Is it behind the iguana? Is it next to the newspaper?* Learners continue to play the game in pairs, taking turns to 'hide' and 'find' the key.

H Ask and answer questions.

- In open class, look at the question prompts about Helen's text message. Write on the board *Who ……… from?* In L1, remind learners they make the question by adding words where the slashes are. Point to the gaps and ask *What's this question?* (**Who** is Helen's text **from?**)

- Learners expand the other notes in the same way. Write the five questions on the board.

- Divide learners into A and B pairs. Learner A holds the book as normal. Learner B holds the book upside down to read the task. Ask one pair to demonstrate this. Learner A asks questions about Helen's text. Learner B answers. Learner B then asks about Dan's text and Learner A answers.

- Feed back in open class. Ask A learners to talk about Helen's text. Ask B learners to talk about Dan's text.

Test tip: FLYERS
Speaking (Part 2)

✔ In this information exchange task, learners are given five prompts to help them form questions to ask the examiner and five answers to the examiner's questions. Remind learners how to use the prompts to form their questions, e.g. *What/about* and *Long/short* can be expanded in this task to **What** *was the message* **about**? *Was the message* **long** *or* **short**? Learners hear the examiner asking these questions first, so they should listen carefully and copy them.

➜ Invent a situation in open class about, e.g. a birthday party. Avoid future scenarios. Write prompts (and chosen answers) on the board, e.g. *When/party – Tuesday, What/do – played games, Fun/boring – fun.* Give learners practice in expanding the prompts in open class. Pairs then take turns to ask and answer the questions.

Let's have fun!

Perform the play called *Summer fun* from Unit 8.

Learners look at page 71, Activity 8. Ask *What are these classmates doing in the picture?* (acting out the play)

Learners read the points below and begin to plan their performance. If possible, the class sits in a circle to discuss the play.

Before beginning to practise and organise the performance, discuss the script together. In open class, ask *What changes do you want to make to the play? Do you want to add any scenes? Do you want to introduce more characters? Do you want Mr Whistle to talk?*

Talk about the different jobs involved in producing a play. Write possible roles up on the board, e.g.

- *Play writers who choose the words the actors will say*

- *Directors who give actors instructions*

- *Costume designers who draw and find or make clothes for the characters*

- *Set designers who find props and organise the stage*

- *Designers for the tickets and posters to advertise the play*

- *Actors*

Involve the whole class in the play, giving everyone a role. You could also nominate some students to video the play, using a phone or tablet. Give each learner a copy of Photocopy 8 (TB page 61). Learners use these to design their costumes and stage. Learners can use props such as a box of crayons, a mobile phone, a sketch pad and a bunch of grapes, if these are available.

Learners take time to practise the play and get costumes, props and posters ready. They perform the play for another class or for parents.

8 *Let's speak!*

What are you interested in? Ask and answer and say why.

Ask *What was Helen interested in in the play?* (iguanas, eagles, foxes, dinosaurs, racing cars, exciting jobs, mangoes, cat food, etc.)

Learners then look at page 73, Activity 8. Ask two learners to role play the conversation.

Say *You can say sports that you like, animals, foods, hobbies, music, films or school subjects, for example.* You could write these topics on the board, to help learners with ideas.

The two learners complete the role play.

Learners then mingle with the rest of the class, taking turns to ask and answer the question.

Ask learners to tell the class what they or their partners are interested in, e.g. *Lucy is interested in playing hockey and reading about history. She likes history because it is exciting.*

Ask *What is this class most interested in?* (e.g. This class is most interested in dinosaurs at the moment.)

 Let's say! Page 75

31 Say *Look at page 75, Activity 8. Listen.* Play the audio. Say *Let's say /z/. Katy's, cousin, amazing, zebra, plays, wins, prizes, design, clothes, kangaroos.* Learners repeat.
Say *Tell me more English words with /z/.* Learners answer (e.g. zoo, Zoe, zero). Learners listen again to the audio, repeating the rhyme as fast as they can.

Home FUN booklet

➡ **Pages 20–21, work**
➡ **Picture dictionary: work**

Go online

to practise your English
to listen to the audio recordings
to find more FUN activities!

2

I never eat that!

Complete the time words.

Then colour the boxes. Each box is a day of the week. How many days of the week should you colour for each word?

	Monday	Tuesday	Wednesday	Thursday	Friday	Saturday	Sunday
n _ _ _ _							
s _ _ _ _ _ _ _ _							
o _ _ _ _							
u _ _ _ _ _ _							
a _ _ _ _ _							

Answer the questions.

Which food do you never eat?   ....

What do you sometimes drink?   ....

Who do you often talk to?   ....

Where do you usually sit in your home? ....

What do you always do at night?   ....

Feelings

Feelings

My animal fact file

....

....

....

....

....

....

....

5 One day, I'd like to ...

win a competition!

swim with dolphins!

be a famous footballer!

help other people!

write books!

ride a camel!

climb a very high mountain!

be on television!

study at university!

be a film star!

live in another country!

go around the world!

be very rich!

go shark fishing!

be a doctor!

live in the jungle!

learn to ski!

go to the moon!

work in a circus!

have lots of children!

My name is .... and one day, I'd like to

....

....

....

This is me! ➡

Jobs

6

My new drink

Our play

1 Design costumes for your play.

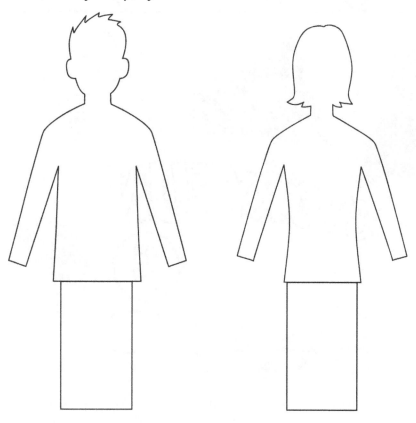

2 Design the scene for your stage.

STORYFUN
5

To: ....

Name of school: ....

Date: ....

Signed: ....

Well done!

PHOTOCOPIABLE © Cambridge University Press and UCLES 2017

Audio track listing

01　　Title and copyright

02　　The village party

03　　The village party F

04　　Ben's wishes

05　　Ben's wishes D

06　　Treasure

07　　Treasure E

08　　Treasure G

09　　Treasure I

10　　The king's colours

11　　The king's colours E

12　　The king's colours G

13　　The king's colours I

14　　Robert's envelopes

15　　Robert's envelopes H

16　　Lara and the mountain lion

17　　Lara and the mountain lion E

18　　Lara and the mountain lion H

19　　Lara and the mountain lion I

20　　Harry's diary

21　　Harry's diary F

22　　Summer fun

23　　Summer fun G

24　　Let's say! 1

25　　Let's say! 2

26　　Let's say! 3

27　　Let's say! 4

28　　Let's say! 5

29　　Let's say! 6

30　　Let's say! 7

31　　Let's say! 8

Acknowledgements

The author would like to acknowledge the shared professionalism and FUN she's experienced whilst working with colleagues during 20 years of production of YLE tests. She would also like to thank CUP for their support in the writing of this second edition of *Storyfun*.
On a personal note, Karen fondly thanks her inspirational story-telling grandfather, and now, three generations later, her sons, Tom and Will, for adding so much creative fun to our continuation of the family story-telling and story-making tradition.

Design and typeset by Wild Apple Design.

Cover design and header artwork by Nicholas Jackson (Astound).

Sound recordings by Hart McLeod, Cambridge.

Music by Mark Fishlock and produced by Ian Harker. Recorded at The Soundhouse Studios, London.

The authors and publishers acknowledge the following sources of copyright material and are grateful for the permissions granted. While every effort has been made, it has not always been possible to identify the sources of all the material used, or to trace all copyright holders. If any omissions are brought to our notice, we will be happy to include the appropriate acknowledgements on reprinting.

The authors and publishers are grateful to the following illustrators:

Key: BC = Bottom Centre; BL = Bottom Left; BR = Bottom Right; C = Centre; TC = Top Centre;
TL = Top Left; TR = Top Right
Mark Beech p. 62 (BL)
Galia Bernstein p. 62 (BR)
Beccy Blake c/o Sylvie Poggio Artists Agency p. 62 (BC)
Nigel Dobbyn c/o Beehive Illustration pp. 60, 61
Roland Dry p. 62 (TR)
Isobel Escalante p. 62 (TL)
Clive Goodyer c/o Beehive Illustration pp. 55, 56, 58, 59
Juanbjuan Oliver c/o Beehive Illustration p. 62 (C)
Sarah Warburton p. 62 (TC)